Praying Scripture
for a
CHANGE

An Introduction to Lectio Divina

TIM GRAY

ASCENSION
PRESS

West Chester, Pennsylvania

Nihil obstat: Mr. Francis X. Maier
                  Censor Deputatus

Imprimatur: +Most Reverend Charles J. Chaput, O.F.M. Cap.
                Archbishop of Denver
                December 30, 2008

Ascension Press
Post Office Box 1990
West Chester, PA 19380
Orders: 1-800-376-0520
BibleStudyforCatholics.com
AscensionPress.com

Cover design: Devin Schadt

Printed in the United States of America
13 8 7 6

ISBN 978-1-934217-48-1

To my students at St. John Vianney Seminary and at the Augustine Institute:

Thank you for deepening my desire to teach, write, and pray.

Contents

Acknowledgments

This project began several years ago when Fr. Michael Glenn and Fr. Chris Hellstrom asked me to teach Scripture for the men in the Spirituality Year at St. John Vianney Seminary. This year-long course gave me a new challenge, to teach Scripture spiritually and not just academically. The challenge proved an immense blessing to me, leading me to study the rich tradition of *lectio divina*. I was inspired to speak and teach more widely on the art of praying with Scripture, and feedback from students and parishioners encouraged me to take up the task of writing my thoughts into the book you are now holding. I want to extend my sincere thanks to Frs. Glenn and Hellstrom for giving me the honor and opportunity to teach *lectio divina*.

I also want to thank my good friends Jeff Cavins, Sarah Christmyer, and Matthew Pinto for their encouragement and support for this project. Special thanks to several friends, Mark Shea, Thomas Smith, and Sean Innerst, who helped edit and comment on the drafts of this book; their feedback was invaluable. Most of all, I want to thank my literal in-house editor, my dear wife, Kris. She is a fabulous editor, and I am grateful that she works so hard to improve my writing and my life—thanks for sharing the adventure!

Biblical Abbreviations

The following abbreviations are used for the various Scriptural verses cited throughout the book. (Note: CCC = Catechism of the Catholic Church.)

Old Testament

Gn	Genesis
Ex	Exodus
Lv	Leviticus
Nm	Numbers
Dt	Deuteronomy
Jos	Joshua
Jgs	Judges
Ru	Ruth
1 Sam	1 Samuel
2 Sam	2 Samuel
1 Kgs	1 Kings
2 Kgs	2 Kings
1 Chr	1 Chronicles
2 Chr	2 Chronicles
Ezr	Ezra
Neh	Nehemiah
Tb	Tobit
Jdt	Judith
Est	Esther
1 Mc	1 Maccabees
2 Mc	2 Maccabees
Jb	Job
Ps	Psalms
Prv	Proverbs
Eccl	Ecclesiastes
Sng	Song of Songs
Wis	Wisdom
Sir	Sirach
Is	Isaiah
Jer	Jeremiah
Lam	Lamentations
Bar	Baruch
Ez	Ezekiel
Dn	Daniel
Hos	Hosea
Jl	Joel
Am	Amos
Ob	Obadiah
Jon	Jonah
Mi	Micah
Na	Nahum
Hb	Habakkuk
Zep	Zephaniah
Hg	Haggai
Zec	Zechariah
Mal	Malachi

New Testament

Mt	Matthew
Mk	Mark
Lk	Luke
Jn	John
Acts	Acts
Rom	Romans
1 Cor	1 Corinthians
2 Cor	2 Corinthians
Gal	Galatians
Eph	Ephesians
Phil	Philippians
Col	Colossians
1 Thess	1 Thessalonians
2 Thess	2 Thessalonians
1 Tm	1 Timothy
2 Tm	2 Timothy
Ti	Titus
Phlm	Philemon
Heb	Hebrews
Jas	James
1 Pt	1 Peter
2 Pt	2 Peter
1 Jn	1 John
2 Jn	2 John
3 Jn	3 John
Jude	Jude
Rv	Revelation

Introduction

The Problem of Prayer

Well, let's now at any rate come clean. Prayer is irksome. An excuse
to omit it is never unwelcome. When it is over, this casts a feeling of
relief and holiday over the rest of the day. We are reluctant to begin. We
are delighted to finish. While we are at prayer, but not while we are
reading a novel or solving a crossword puzzle, any trifle is enough
to distract us. And we know that we are not alone in this.

— C.S. Lewis

Yes, indeed. We are not alone in finding prayer difficult. I have often found it irksome, too. More times than I would like to admit I have looked at prayer as a burden, something to be checked off my "to do" list, like washing the dishes or flossing my teeth; something that I know I should do daily but all too often regard as a duty.

The necessity of prayer is seared into the Christian conscience, and yet many of us live our lives short on prayer. We hear the Bible call us to "pray without ceasing" (1 Thess 5:17). We hear stories of saints who seemed to talk with God as easily as placing a direct call, and we erroneously imagine that prayer was effortless for them, marked always with joy, consolation, voices, and visions. Against this backdrop we grow discouraged, convincing ourselves that we must have been born missing some "mystic gene."

The stark contrast between the saints who heard God speak and us who often hear only our rosaries clacking against the pew was brought home to me in a rather surprising way one night as I was tucking my son, Joseph, into bed. After bedtime prayers, he burst into tears, crying "God doesn't talk to me." A spiritual crisis at age four! He was upset because God didn't talk to him the way He talked to Jonah or St. Francis. No visions or voices! He thought something was wrong with him.

A lot of people feel like Joseph. While they might not expect visions or voices, they find prayer dry, confusing, frustrating, or just plain hard. Prayer is one of the fundamental marks of the spiritual life, as basic to Christian life as baseball and apple pie is to American identity. But when we look at our own feeble efforts at prayer we wonder how in the world we can listen to God, much less know and do His will.

What's the Matter with Us?

If you have trouble praying, then welcome to the human race. The fact is, we don't know *how* to pray. Everybody, including the saints, begins life not knowing how to pray. Don't take my word for it. Read what the apostle Paul tells us in Romans 8:26, "We do not know how to pray as we ought."

The problem is not that we are exceptionally bad at prayer compared to other people. The problem is that we are normal— which is to say, we are afflicted with the results of original sin. Our first parents enjoyed unbroken communion with God (shown in the book of Genesis by the image of God "walking in the garden" with Adam and Eve, speaking with them freely and they with Him). With original sin, however, everything changed. The imagery of Genesis is vivid and profound. God doesn't hide from us; in fact, He comes looking for us. But we hide from God (see Gn 3:8), our sin and shame opening a gulf between God and man and shattering the communion of "the beginning." More than that, sin brought pain, backbreaking work, fruitless longing, domination, strife, and death into the world, breaking not only our relationship with God and but also with each other (Gn 3:16-19). Sin results in a darkened mind, a weakened will, and disordered desires (i.e., concupiscence). And as these maladies play out over time, we lose sight of God altogether.

Bridging the chasm between Creator and creature is no simple matter. God Himself observes the distance between us, saying, "For my thoughts are not your thoughts, neither are your ways my ways, says the LORD. For as the heavens are higher than the earth, so are my ways higher than your ways and my thoughts than your thoughts" (Is 55:8-9). Given how difficult it is to have a deep, constant and committed relationship with another person, we should not be surprised that it is not easy to attempt a relationship with God, who is "wholly other." The very idea of bridging the gap between God and humanity seems beyond improbable, so much so that the ancient Greek philosophers concluded that God and humanity could not be friends, because they were so unlike.

A Bridge over Troubled Waters

Have you ever met someone with whom you share nothing in common? It makes conversation rather difficult, if not downright impossible. When you meet someone for the first time, there is always that initial awkwardness in a first conversation. Once you move beyond small talk about the weather and geographical origins you either find some common ground, some shared interest that becomes the subject of conversation, or the conversation runs out of steam.

Recently, I met someone for a business luncheon. During our introductory small talk we discovered that we shared something in common, something deeply important to both of us: we each have an only child who is adopted. As we shared our adoption stories we found them strikingly similar and had a very lively conversation. This conversation created a connection that sowed the seeds for an ongoing friendship. If our conversation had consisted only of small talk, it would have been like a fire fed only with small twigs and kindling, which doesn't have the intensity to last very long.

This highlights one of the difficulties of prayer. If deep conversation begins with sharing something in common, what could we sinful human beings have in common with the Creator of the universe? What makes us think we could sit down and have a conversation with God that could lead to friendship?

This seemingly insurmountable problem, however, was overcome when "the Word of God became flesh and dwelt among us" (Jn 1:14). God became man, calling us His "friends" (Jn 15:14). In the Incarnation, when the Second Person of the Trinity took on human nature, something utterly astonishing and unexpected happened. The gap between creature and Creator was bridged, with Jesus taking a form that is "lower than the angels" (Heb 2:9) in order that He might call us "brethren" (Heb 2:11). Thus, as the author of Hebrews joyfully declares:

> Since then we have a great high priest who has passed
> through the heavens, Jesus, the Son of God, let us hold

fast our confession. For we have not a high priest who is unable to sympathize with our weaknesses, but one who in every respect has been tempted as we are, yet without sinning. Let us then with confidence draw near to the throne of grace, that we may receive mercy and find grace to help in time of need (Heb 4:14-16).

We share more in common with God than the greatest philosophers could ever have imagined. Jesus took on our nature to bridge the gap caused by sin and to restore the communion lost by original sin. As the *Catechism of the Catholic Church* so eloquently puts it, "Man may forget his Creator or hide far from His face ... yet the living and true God tirelessly calls each person to that mysterious encounter known as prayer" (CCC 2567). And as we shall see, in the person of Jesus, God not only calls us but brings us into friendship with Him and teaches us how to pray.

Christ Our Teacher

Like St. Paul (and us), the twelve apostles were aware that they didn't know how to pray. This is why they went to Jesus and asked "Lord, teach us to pray" (Lk 11:1-4). Notice that Jesus did not scold them for not knowing how to pray, tell them prayer was a snap, advise them to just go with the flow, or tell them that whatever popped into their heads was the voice of God. Sympathetic to human weakness, Jesus taught them how to pray, both by His example and His teaching.

In the Old Testament, God revealed His pedagogy on prayer when He created for Israel two great sanctuaries in which to encounter Him: the Sabbath and the Temple. The Sabbath was the sanctuary in time. From the moment of creation, God called His people to set aside their temporal concerns and labors, and enter into the rest and refreshment of worship. The Sabbath, the twenty-four-hour period from sundown to sundown at the end of each week, was "made for man," as Jesus says in Mark 2:27; made so that man and woman might not forget that their ultimate happiness would not be found in the fruit of the field, but in relationship with God, which is the fruit of worship and prayer.

Whereas the Sabbath was God's sanctuary in time, the Temple was His sanctuary in space. Within the Temple dwelt the very presence of God. It was to the Temple that God's people came to offer sacrifice and receive the Lord's mercy. In the Tent of Meeting, the predecessor to the Temple, Moses talked to the LORD "face to face" (Ex 33:11). Until God Himself would come and walk on the earth, the Temple was the singular place of intimate encounter with God. These two sanctuaries were a continual reminder and invitation to God's people to set apart space and time for union with the Lord.

In the gospels, Jesus modeled this practice of setting aside a sanctuary in time and space for the Father. The gospels are full of moments where we observe Jesus engaged in the relationship we call prayer. He prays at pivotal moments such as His baptism (Lk 3:21) and the selection of the twelve apostles (Lk 6:12-16). We find Him at prayer in the glory of the Mount of Transfiguration (Lk 9:28-29) and the darkness of Gethsemane and Calvary (Mt 26:36-39; Lk 23:34, 46). He prays in public, at the synagogue in Nazareth (Lk 4:16) and at the Temple in Jerusalem (Lk 2:45-49), and in private. Mark tells us that Jesus got up early in the morning and sought out lonely places to pray (Mk 1:35). Matthew and Luke recount that Jesus prayed into the evening and through the night and sought out places to be with His Father in heaven (see Mt 14:23, Lk 6:12-13). The apostles acquired this habit, and so we read that "all these with one accord devoted themselves to prayer" (Acts 1:14) and that "Peter and John were going up to the temple at the hour of prayer, the ninth hour" (Acts 3:1; see also Lk 24:53).

Jesus' habit of prayer, His preaching, and His answer to the apostles' request, all emphasize the truth that *God teaches us to pray.* As the *Catechism of the Catholic Church* notes, our response to the Teacher should be to "approach the Lord Jesus as Moses approached the burning bush: first to contemplate him in prayer, then to hear how he teaches us to pray" (CCC 2598).

Indeed, the crucial thing for us to understand is that God is eager to teach us how to pray. So eager, in fact, that His Spirit is already at work in us creating the "divine discontent" we so often feel about our prayer lives. God does not judge our attempts at prayer any more than a natural father would chide an infant taking his first steps. Rather, He cheers us on, motivates us to try again, and encourages us to seek out and question those wiser and more experienced (see Prv 11:14), to search more deeply, to explore the "wisdom of the ages" in our restless quest.

Prayer and the School of the Holy Spirit

Here, we discover a vital hidden-in-plain-sight secret of the Christian life: *The reason anyone anywhere at any time has ever been moved to pray is because God, by His Spirit, was drawing them toward him.* Jesus says as much when He tells His disciples that "no one can come to me unless the Father who sent me draws him" (Jn 6:44). Every prayer to God that has ever been uttered was uttered at the prompting of the Holy Spirit.

The very desire that inspired the apostles to say, "Teach us to pray" came from God. God desires our dialogue of prayer with Him more than we do. As the *Catechism* observes, "Whether we realize it or not, prayer is the encounter of God's thirst with ours. God thirsts that we may thirst for him" (CCC 2560). That may be hard to believe, since we often feel that our prayer consists primarily of us banging away at the gates of heaven and crying "How long, O Lord." But St. Paul describes in his letter to the Romans how intimately God is involved in our prayer:

> Likewise the Spirit helps us in our weakness; for we do not know how to pray as we ought, but the Spirit himself intercedes for us with sighs too deep for words. And he who searches the hearts of men knows what is the mind of the Spirit, because the Spirit intercedes for the saints according to the will of God (Rom 8:26-27).

In short, God doesn't just teach us how to pray; His Spirit empowers us to pray. He enables us on earth to do what God the Son does eternally: offer the Father praise and thanksgiving for the gift of the Father's love in the Spirit. What we need to realize is that we are never left on our own when it comes to prayer.

This is precisely Paul's point in highlighting the role of the Holy Spirit in prayer. "When we cry, 'Abba! Father!' it is the Spirit himself bearing witness with our spirit that we are children of God" (Rom 8:15-16). Paul knew from experience that Jesus gives us far more than a method of prayer; He gives us the means to pray through His Spirit.

We must always keep in mind that prayer is God's invitation to enter into an intimate relationship of love and life with Him. If we forget that this is what is happening when we pray, we start treating prayer as simply an obligation, as a hoop that must be jumped through in order to avoid offending God and provoking His displeasure. We should never see prayer as a means of bribing, manipulating, or placating a capricious god. Such a view is not only false but ultimately enslaving.

God doesn't want us to be slaves, but free sons and daughters. And so He gives us the liberating Spirit of His Son and showers us with gifts through His Holy Church. Indeed, the *Catechism* defines prayer as a familial relationship: "Christian prayer is a covenant relationship between God and man in Christ" (CCC 2564). God desires a personal relationship with us through our Lord Jesus, who has paid with His blood to open the door for us to enter into that relationship. And that's the good news: the God who calls us to relationship, and who has suffered and died to bridge the chasm between man and God, will surely provide the means for us to enter into this intimate relationship of prayer. The God who has put in your heart the desire to know Him intimately will fulfill that desire.

In the course of this book, we will discover the secret of the saints, an approach to prayer which can enable us to begin the adventure of a life-giving dialogue with God.

Chapter One

The Secret of the Saints

Diligently practice prayer and lectio divina. When you pray,
you speak with God; when you read, God speaks to you."

— St. Cyprian

A friend of mine has a T-shirt he wears as a sort of humorous act of penance. It says, "Help me! I'm talking and I can't shut up!" My friend knows that he has a tendency to rattle on a bit too much and that when this happens something is out of balance. When somebody dominates a conversation, things tend to get dull in a hurry. Monologue is monotonous. This is no small part of what goes wrong with our prayer lives. We cry out, like Samuel, "Speak Lord, your servant is listening" (1 Sam 3:9-10), but often we rarely stop talking long enough to let God get a word in edgewise. When we finally close our eyes, seeking the inner silence that would allow us to hear God's "still small voice" (1 Kngs 19:12), this voice often seems inaudible. When we don't receive what we expect, we feel like giving up. Prayer is a conversation, but we don't know how to enter into that conversation. We monologue until it gets boring, and then, in our fatigue, we give up.

Of course, it is good to express our thanks, needs, fears, pains, joys, and questions to God. Indeed, as we have already observed, the Holy Spirit helps us express our hearts to God. But, as the old saying goes, "It takes two to tango." Our speaking to God is only half the conversation. God has to respond with His part of the dialogue. Jesus teaches us how to address God as Father and Paul encourages us by explaining that the Holy Spirit helps us pray to God, but what about God's part in the conversation? How do we hear God when He is speaking to us?

The Voice of God

The Christian tradition has discerned three ways in which God communicates to us and has elucidated these ways using the metaphor of a book. God first speaks by authoring the book of creation, creating everything with careful design, measure, number, and weight (Wis 11:20). This intricate "penmanship" of creation reveals meaning and a message. The psalmist sings of creation's eternal announcement: "The heavens are telling the glory of God; and the firmament proclaims his handiwork. Day to day pours forth speech, and night to night declares knowledge" (Ps 19:1-2). The psalmist even speaks of creation's "words" going forth to the ends of the world. St. Paul understood that this book of creation could be read, and from it God's "eternal power and deity" (Rom 1:19-20) could clearly be perceived. Similarly, St. Anthony remarked to a questioning philosopher, "My book ... is the nature of things created, and it is present whenever I want to read the words of God."[1] St. Augustine likewise commented that the beauty of creation is a profession of the Beautiful One who created them. And so Augustine, and much of the Christian tradition after him,

---

[1]   Samuel Rubenson, *The Letters of St. Anthony: Monasticism and the Making of a Saint* (Minneapolis: Fortress Press, 1990), p. 159.

concluded that the world itself is God's "book," proclaiming the glory of the Creator.[2]

Unfortunately, due to sin, humanity often misreads the book of the cosmos that God has given us. In fact, we often misread the book of nature so badly that we forget the Author altogether and worship the book, adoring creation instead of the Creator. Herein lies the origin of the world's pagan religions, which contain a sad mixture of longing for God and seeking Him (see Acts 17:22-27) combined with the tendency to worship anything and everything except God (see Rom 1:20-32).

Within this first book of creation, God penned a second and surpassing book, the book of the human person. The human person, made in God's image with an immortal soul and a longing for communion, was created to reflect the one true God, who is also a Triune communion of Divine Persons. With the Fall, however, this divine image became darkened, disjointed, and distorted, like the reflection in a tarnished, shattered mirror. Badly garbled by the Fall, the book of the human person, sometimes called the book of the soul, became a difficult read.

With the effects of original sin distorting both the book of nature and the book of the human person, how can we hear God's communication? The good news is that God gives us another book— the book of divine revelation—which communicates His words to us, allowing us to open the books of creation and the soul and read them correctly. As the *Catechism* reminds us, "By revealing himself God

---

[2]   St. Augustine, *Sermon on Psalm 103*. For additional references and discussion see Yves M.-J. Congar, *Tradition and Traditions* (New York: Macmillan, 1966), pp. 65-66, footnote 2.

wishes to make [us] capable of responding to him, and of knowing him, and of loving him far beyond [our] own natural capacity" (CCC 52). For St. Augustine and the medieval tradition that followed him, God's Word to humanity, addressed through the marvelous books of creation and of the soul, was lost on us due to the deafness and blindness caused by our sin. After the Fall, God continually called out to His people through the patriarchs, judges, and prophets of the Old Covenant, but our sins left us deaf to His call. So, in a last effort, God's Word was made flesh, so that He could heal our deafness and cure our blindness. When the Word became flesh, God's voice at last could be heard by human ears. Only through Jesus can we come to discern and hear clearly God's Word to us.

This Word of Divine Revelation is handed down to us through Scripture and Tradition, which provide us with the Rosetta Stone for deciphering all that God wants to communicate to humanity. God desires to enter into a dialogue with us. As the Second Vatican Council noted, "In the sacred books, the Father who is in heaven comes lovingly to meet his children, and talks to them" (*Dei Verbum*, 21). With His coming, Jesus opens the entire book of Scripture to us, and in turn the Scriptures open up the mystery of God's communication in creation and the soul as well.

A good example of how God speaks in the book of Scripture and opens up the other books of the cosmos and the human person can be seen the life of St. Francis of Assisi. St. Francis heard the Gospel, and his immersion in it not only conformed him to Christ but opened up the meaning of the book of creation. Francis is known for his joy and love of God's creation, but too often people see him as a simple-minded tree hugger. Francis exulted in the beauty of nature because he saw that it, like Scripture itself, is a love letter from our Heavenly Father. For St. Francis, creation was always "telling the glory of God," and so in it he always found an occasion for contemplating the face of God. Francis knew how to hear God's voice in creation, because he first listened to that voice in Scripture.

It is with good reason then that the Church Fathers (such as St. Augustine) and the medieval Doctors (such as St. Thomas Aquinas and St. Bonaventure) saw Scripture as holding a central place in Christian life. The lesson behind all this is simple but profound: the normative way God speaks to His people is through His Word, especially in the Holy Scriptures.

The Secret of the Saints Opens a Closed Book

Even though we may be aware of the importance of the Bible, many of us still find it a closed book. One of the difficulties in opening this sacred book is seeing it as the Word of God, a word that is addressed personally to each of us. When we read the Bible, we can feel like we are reading somebody else's mail. Much of the Scriptures seem to be addressed to someone else at another time and place. God speaks to specific individuals such as Moses, Joshua, Deborah, David, Solomon, Mary, Peter, and Paul. He sends oracles to nations such as Israel, Babylon, and Egypt, and even to obscure peoples such as Edom and Assyria. No matter how thoroughly we read the Bible, we do not find our own name written on the page. And as the great philosopher Ludwig Wittgenstein keenly observed, "You can't hear God speak to someone else, you can hear him only if you are being addressed."[3]

---

[3] Ludwig Wittgenstein, *Zettel* (Oxford: Blackwell, 1967), p. 717.

How are we to open this holy book to meet the Lord and hear Him speak to us? The answer is one of the true secrets of the saints. The saints didn't have some mystic gene in their DNA, but they did share with St. Paul an insight that he had eagerly taught the first Christians: Scripture is living and active, and so it ever remains God's Word spoken to whomever has the courage to pick it up and receive it. The letter to the Hebrews describes the power of God's Word this way: "For the word of God is living and active, sharper than any two-edged sword, piercing to the division of soul and spirit, of joints and marrow, and discerning the thoughts and intentions of the heart" (Heb 4:12). And, as Paul tells the Romans, "For whatever was written in former days was written for our instruction, that by steadfastness and by the encouragement of the scriptures we might have hope" (Rom 15:4). Paul's point is profound, Scripture was not written down simply for the people who figure in it, like Moses and Peter, but it was also written for those of us who follow the God of Moses and Peter.

St. Paul reiterates this understanding when he teaches the Corinthians that the history of Israel was written down not simply to record events, but because it is pertinent first and foremost to all Christians. "Now these things happened to them as a warning, but they were written down for our instruction" (1 Cor 10:11). Paul's point is simple: you, not just Israel, are the one being addressed in Scripture. This makes a tremendous difference for us reading the Scriptures today. It is the difference between picking up a letter and thinking it is addressed to someone else versus realizing that it is intended for you. God's Word is ever ancient, ever new.

This is why Scripture cannot be locked in the past. Pope Benedict XVI argues, "But of course a mere historical reading of the Bible is not enough. We do not read it as the former words of humans; we read it as the word of God always present in a new way that was given to all ages through the people of a past age. To lodge this word solely in the past means to deny the Bible as Bible."[4] Thus, Scripture is a word that always transcends its original moment in time, for its voice continues to go out to all generations.

God's voice in the Scriptures is not an ancient news report about something that occurred in a long-forgotten past. Nor is Scripture a form letter sent out in a generic mass mailing. Rather, it is a personal note addressed to each of us, intended to speak personally to the intimate details of our life.

During our engagement, my wife and I were living on different sides of the country. The separation prompted many late-night phone calls and letters and notes continually mailed and sent off across the miles. As I returned home from teaching each day, I looked forward with excitement to the possibility of finding a new letter waiting for me in the mailbox, which I would immediately open and read with delight. A lover who is separated from the beloved doesn't let a love letter just sit on the kitchen table unopened for days on end with the ever-growing pile of junk mail, but instead quickly and eagerly opens it upon its arrival, reading and re-reading it until the ink is nearly worn off from use. Scripture is a love letter from our Divine Bridegroom, and, like the saints, we too should eagerly and often read the Scriptures and hear there the voice our Beloved speaking to us.

---

[4] Joseph Cardinal Ratzinger, *A New Song for the Lord: Faith in Christ and Liturgy Today* (New York: Crossroad, 1997), pp. 170-71.

Take and Read

This "secret," that God speaks directly to each of us in His Word, changed many sinners into holy saints. St. Augustine was the original well-to-do playboy. He had studied rhetoric and sought wisdom in various philosophies and happiness in a liaison with a concubine, but found nothing that satisfied his heart. Eventually, he met St. Ambrose of Milan, who first made Scripture accessible to him. He found himself attracted to Christianity but could not make the jump, famously praying "O Lord, make me chaste. But not yet." His spiritual journey (helped along by the prayers of his devoted mother, St. Monica) eventually reached a crisis point at which he nearly despaired. Augustine recounts how a friend told him the story of St. Anthony's conversion, a story that sparked in Augustine a deeper desire to follow Jesus radically.

St. Anthony was an Egyptian born in the middle of the third century. He was from a wealthy family, and while still a young man he inherited a rather large fortune when his parents died. Wondering what to do with his life and his newfound wealth, he went to a church. Upon entering he heard the gospel reading, "If you would be perfect, go, sell what you possess and give to the poor, and you will have treasure in heaven; and come, follow me" (Mt 19:21). Although these words of Jesus were addressed to the rich young man, Anthony received them as spoken to himself.

He immediately sold everything he had and gave it to the poor, and devoted himself exclusively to Christ. He went out into the desert to live as a hermit and, paradoxically, founded a great movement in the Church (i.e., the Desert Fathers) when a flood of disciples persisted in coming to him for spiritual guidance. By his obedience to the Word of God, he became the father of the entire monastic tradition. The desolate desert became a spiritually fertile land, as Anthony continued to listen attentively each day to Scripture as God's Word addressed to him: this was the lesson he taught to those who likewise left the noise of the world in order to better hear and live God's Word.

Spurred on by the example of St. Anthony, and by many others who had come to faith and God's service as a result of Anthony's life, Augustine began to weep at his own slowness of heart. At that moment, Augustine heard what sounded like the voice of a child singing a refrain over and over again "*tolle lege, tolle lege,*" which means "take and read, take and read." Augustine recounts what happened next:

> I stemmed the flood of tears and rose to my feet, believing that this could be nothing other than a divine command to open the Book and read the first passage I chanced upon; for I had heard the story of how Anthony had been instructed by a gospel text. He happened to arrive while the gospel was being read, *and took the words to be addressed to himself* when he heard, "Go and sell all you possess and give the money to the poor: you will have treasure in heaven. Then come, follow me." So he promptly converted to You by this plainly divine message. Stung into action, I returned to the place where Alypius was sitting, for on leaving it I had put down there the book of the Apostle's letters. I snatched it up, opened it and read in silence the passage on which my eyes first lighted.[5]

Augustine, like Anthony, read a passage from Scripture (Rom 13:11-14) and heard the summons to "put on the Lord Jesus Christ"

---

[5]   St. Augustine, *The Confessions*, Book 8.29, translated by Maria Boulding, O.S.B. (New York: Vintage Books, 1997), p. 168, emphasis added.

as a word spoken directly to him by God. It was the turning point of his life and he fully responded.

Augustine had heard Scripture many times before, but had not converted. His reading of Romans 13 was the first time he heard Scripture as a word personally addressed to *him*, and it transformed his life. As Wittgenstein wisely noted, "you can't hear God speak to someone else, you can hear him only if you are being addressed."[6] This is the secret of the saints; to discover that you are, in fact, being addressed by God in Scripture.

St. Francis of Assisi also discovered this "secret" of God's Word. One day, while Francis was at Mass, the Gospel of the day was read:

> And preach as you go, saying, "The kingdom of heaven is at hand." Heal the sick, raise the dead, cleanse lepers, cast out demons. You received without paying, give without pay. Take no gold, nor silver, nor copper in your belts, no bag for your journey, nor two tunics, nor sandals, nor a staff; for the laborer deserves his food (Mt 10:7-10).

Francis heard these words as spoken directly to himself, and when Mass was over he threw away what little he had left of this world, such as his shoes, cloak, staff, and empty wallet. He donned a coarse woolen tunic, the clothing of peasants, with a knotted rope for a belt and immediately began to exhort the people of the countryside to penance, love, and peace.

The great—and simple—secret of the saints is that they realized that God's Word was addressed to *them*.

---

6   Ludwig Wittgenstein, *Zettel* (Oxford: Blackwell, 1967), p. 717.

Conversing with Jesus

That God is able and desires to speak directly in our life and prayer is not only a secret taught by St. Paul and experienced by the saints; it is revealed throughout the pages of Scripture. Jesus demonstrates this personal encounter when He meets His disciples on the road to Emmaus. Luke begins his account of this event:

> That very day two of them were going to a village named Emmaus, about seven miles from Jerusalem, and talking with each other about all these things that had happened. While they were talking and discussing together, Jesus himself drew near and went with them. But their eyes were kept from recognizing him. And he said to them, "What is this conversation which you are holding with each other as you walk?" And they stood still, looking sad. Then one of them, named Cleopas, answered him, "Are you the only visitor to Jerusalem who does not know the things that have happened there in these days?" And he said to them, "What things?" And they said to him, "Concerning Jesus of Nazareth, who was a prophet mighty in deed and word before God and all the people, and how our chief priests and rulers delivered him up to be condemned to death, and crucified him. But we had hoped that he was the one to redeem Israel. Yes, and besides all this, it is now the third day since this happened. Moreover, some women of our company amazed us. They were at the tomb early in the morning and did not find his body; and they came back saying that they had even seen a vision of angels, who said that he was alive. Some of those who were with us went to the tomb, and found it just as the women had said; but him they did not see" (Lk 24:13-24).

Several things are happening here to which we should pay close attention. First, we see the disciples speaking to Jesus, telling Him their hopes and fears, pouring out their hearts to Him; this is half the dialogue of prayer. It is interesting to note that, as is often the case with our own prayer, these disciples don't really understand that God is listening to them with complete attention and utmost intimacy. God is hidden from them in the very moment when He is in their midst. Sometimes we experience this feeling during our prayer: we feel God is far away and has abandoned us at the very moment when God is closest to us.

> And he said to them, "O foolish men, and slow of heart to believe all that the prophets have spoken! Was it not necessary that the Christ should suffer these things and enter into his glory?" And beginning with Moses and all the prophets, he interpreted to them in all the scriptures the things concerning himself (Lk 24:25-27).

The next thing to note is that Jesus, who is called "Emmanuel" or "God with us" answers His disciples *through Scripture.* He refers them to the testimony of God's Word in the writings of Moses and the prophets and chides them for not really seeing what these writings are saying. He insists that these books (which, to the eyes of the disciples appear to have nothing whatsoever to do with the suffering and death of Jesus, nor with their own suffering and pain) are in fact all about the death and resurrection of Jesus—and therefore have everything to do with answering the deepest questions that are troubling the disciples' hearts at this very moment in their lives.

> So they drew near to the village to which they were going. [Jesus] appeared to be going further, but they constrained

him, saying, "Stay with us, for it is toward evening and the day is now far spent." So he went in to stay with them. When he was at table with them, he took the bread and blessed, and broke it, and gave it to them. And their eyes were opened and they recognized him; and he vanished out of their sight. They said to each other, "Did not our hearts burn within us while he talked to us on the road, while he opened to us the scriptures?" (Lk 24:28-32)

The disciples invite Jesus to stay, and this leads to their full encounter with Christ as He repeats His absolutely distinctive Eucharistic gesture of taking bread, giving thanks, breaking the bread, and giving it to His disciples. It is through the Word of God in union with the Eucharist that their eyes are finally opened and they recognize the Risen Christ.

It all began with Jesus walking and talking with these two disciples, just as God had walked and talked in the Garden with Adam and Eve. Jesus' dialogue breathed new life into the writings of Moses and the prophets, and that personal dialogue with the living God lit a fire in the hearts of these followers of Christ. Jesus takes the words of Scripture and opens the eyes of His disciples to how God's Word applies to and answers the current struggle of their lives. This dialogue with the Living Word Himself, and with His word in the Scriptures, kindled in the hearts of the disciples a burning love that desired union with the Lord. They do not want Jesus to leave; they want to stay with Him. And so dialogue leads to communion. Jesus responds to their invitation to stay with them, which leads not just to a temporal meal, but to an intimate encounter with God Himself, here in the Eucharistic communion in the breaking of the bread. Likewise, the aim of all prayer is an intimate communion with Christ.

The Divine Dialogue

Scripture opens up for us the other half of the dialogue of prayer. Indeed, this was always the ancient Christian perspective on prayer. Listen to how several of the Church Fathers explain this: St. Ambrose, "We speak to Him when we pray; we listen to Him when we read the divine oracles"[7]; St. Augustine, "Your prayer is your word addressed to God. When you read the Bible, God speaks to you; when you pray you speak to God"[8]; St. Cyprian, "Diligently practice prayer and *lectio divina*. When you pray, you speak with God; when you read, God speaks to you."[9] An amazing pattern emerges, "prayer" is how we speak to God, and reading Sacred Scripture is the way we hear God speak to us. In other words, you don't need a mystic gene or divine epiphany to hear God, what you need is to take up the Bible and read.

---

[7]   St. Ambrose, *De Officiis Ministrorum* 1, 20 88: PL 16, 50.
[8]   St. Augustine, *Ennarratio in Ps 85:7*: CCL 39, 1177.
[9]   St. Cyprian, *Ad Donatum,* 15: CCL IIIA, 12.

Chapter Two

Lectio Divina — Stairway to Heaven

The Word of God is the first source of all Christian spirituality. It gives rise to a personal relationship with the living God and with His saving and sanctifying will. It is for this reason that from the very beginning ... what is called lectio divina has been held in the highest regard. By means of it the Word of God is brought to bear on life, on which it projects the light of that wisdom which is a gift of the Spirit.

— Pope John Paul II

W e have looked at the problem of prayer and revealed the secret of the saints (take and read!), but how do we begin to do it? Within the walls of the ancient monasteries a fruitful and powerful process was developed to help us all dialogue with God's Word.

Lectio Divina: The Four-Rung Ladder

Contrary to what many believe, monastic life did not consist simply of prayer. The monks supported themselves and the small villages that formed around them by cultivating the soil, raising animals, and producing some of the finest wines and beers in all of Europe. Each day revolved around three indispensable activities: physical work, liturgical participation, and personal prayer. From these activities developed the monastic motto *Ora et Labora*—"Pray and Work." The monks' physical labors were often focused on the attentive cultivation of the land, while their prayer (both liturgical and personal) was focused on the attentive cultivation of their souls.

In their spiritual endeavor they took up a tool that broke open the fallow fields of Scripture and the even harder ground of the human heart; this tool was the method of prayer known as *lectio divina*. *Lectio* (Latin for "a reading") *divina* ("divine") literally means "divine reading," and refers to the reading of Sacred Scripture in the context of personal prayer.

One of the most popular works on *lectio divina* was written by a Carthusian monk named Guigo, who prayed and worked in and around one of the scenic mountain valleys of the French Alps, at the famous Carthusian motherhouse, the Grande Chartreuse. Many probably had never heard of this ancient sanctuary of prayer, still in existence today, until it was the subject of a documentary film that has become a phenomenon across both Europe and the U.S. This richly artistic work was called *Into Great Silence*. Its director, Philip Gröning, spent six months at this historic monastery, which is normally closed to visitors, collecting footage for his film. Though the screen time is more than two and a half hours, it is filmed in almost complete silence, the primary exception being the monks' chanting the Divine Office. This silence reflects the lives of the monks who follow the Carthusian monastic tradition, living in silence the majority of their day.

The surprising popular response to this award-winning film speaks not only to the spiritual magnetism of this holy monastery, but more importantly to the deep spiritual hunger of our time. It was within this "great silence" that Guigo long ago took the already common practice of *lectio divina* and illuminated it. His reflections are largely found in his classic work on prayer, *Ladder of Monks*, which described with masterful insight four simple steps for praying with Scripture. Guigo begins his book recounting his deepening understanding of the pattern of prayer so central to his daily life:

> One day when I was busy working with my hands I began to think about our spiritual work, and all at once four stages in spiritual exercise came into my mind: reading, meditation, prayer, and contemplation. These make a ladder for monks by which they are lifted up from earth to heaven. It has few rungs, yet its length is immense and wonderful, for its lower end rests upon the earth, but its top pierces the clouds and touches heavenly secrets.[10]

Like the others in his tradition, Guigo kept silence even as he labored with his hands, allowing even his time of physical labor to provide an occasion for spiritual meditation. The fruit of Guigo's labors proved not only to be a help to his own prayer, but will also prove a gift to our prayer as well. In fact, Guigo's description of *lectio divina* is quoted in the fourth pillar of the *Catechism*, where it is invoked as a model for praying with Scripture (CCC 2654).

Icon of the Spiritual Life

At the center of Guigo's method is the metaphor of a ladder that reaches to heaven. The image of a ladder was an ancient symbol for spiritual ascent, with deep roots in the Judeo-Christian tradition. The origins of this tradition are to be found in the book of Genesis, in the story of Jacob's dream about a ladder that extended from earth to heaven.

---

[10] Guigo the Carthusian, *Guigo II: Ladder of Monks and Twelve Meditations* (Kalamazoo, MI: Cistercian Publications, 1979), pp. 67-68.

In Genesis 28, Abraham's grandson Jacob found himself far from home and alone. Wandering north on a road that would take him to his mother's family, Jacob wondered whether he would ever return to the Promised Land again. Tired and exhausted, he fell asleep, and experienced a startling vision from God:

> And he came to a certain place, and stayed there that night, because the sun had set. Taking one of the stones of the place, he put it under his head and lay down in that place to sleep. *And he dreamed that there was a ladder set up on the earth, and the top of it reached to heaven; and behold, the angels of God were ascending and descending on it* (Gn 28:11-12, emphasis added).

Upon waking from the dream Jacob exclaimed, "'Surely the Lord is in this place; and I did not know it.' And he was afraid, and said, 'How awesome is this place! This is none other than the house of God, and this is the gate of heaven'" (Gn 28:16-17). The name for "house of God" in Hebrew is *Bethel*, which became the name of the place where Jacob saw the ladder. The later rabbinic tradition claimed that the Temple in Jerusalem was the true Bethel, since it was the ultimate house of God, where heaven and earth intersected and where all the angels ascend and descend between earth and heaven. Thus, the rabbinic tradition spiritually relocated Jacob's Bethel from the literal city of Bethel in the north of Israel to Jerusalem further south. Jerusalem, however, is not the last stop for Bethel and the stairway to heaven.

St. John records that Jesus referred to this very incident in the life of Jacob when he declared to Nathanael, "Truly, truly, I say to you, you will see heaven opened, and the angels of God ascending and descending upon the Son of man" (Jn 1:51). Jesus' words to

Nathanael seem rather odd if they are not read in light of the Jewish tradition concerning Jacob's ladder. Just as the rabbinic tradition relocated Bethel to Jerusalem, Jesus' seemingly strange words to Nathanael relocate Bethel once again. The true connection between heaven and earth is not to be located in a geographical landmark, but rather in the person of Jesus. Jesus bridges the chasm between earth and heaven, bringing God's presence. Thus, the angels that ascended and descended on Jacob's ladder do so now through the person of Jesus. In Jewish figures of speech Jesus was claiming to be the true and ultimate "Bethel," or house of God. This is what St. John hints at in the prologue to his gospel, when he described how the "Word became flesh and dwelt among us." The Greek verb translated as "dwelt" has the sense of "to pitch one's tent," "to tabernacle," as God tabernacles in the Ark of the Covenant, which was first in the Tent of Meeting and later moved to the Temple. Jesus, in short, is the new Temple—but not one that is stationary, but rather on the move. Jesus is the Way, the Way is a ladder, and one climbs a ladder one step at a time.

Not surprisingly, the Christian tradition has long seen in the image of Jacob's ladder an icon of the spiritual life. Jacob, wandering far from home, encounters God and receives a vision and a promise that God will be with him and provide for his return to the Promised Land. Ancient Christian writers (long before Guigo the Carthusian) such as St. John Climacus used this image as a metaphor for our own journey to heaven, a journey in which we must climb the ladder from earth to heaven. Our prayerful ascent to God must, as the ancient masters of the spiritual life point out, be taken one step at a time.

One Rung at a Time

Guigo believed that the fourfold method of *lectio divina* was like the four rungs of a ladder which, if ascended one rung at a time in proper order, would lead the soul to heaven. Here is one of the ways Guigo described the rungs of this spiritual ladder:

> *Reading* is the careful study of the Scriptures, concentrating all one's powers on it. *Meditation* is the busy application of the mind to seek with the help of one's own reason for knowledge of hidden truth. *Prayer* is the heart's devoted turning to God to drive away evil and obtain what is good. *Contemplation* is when the mind is in some sort lifted up to God and held above itself, so that it tastes the joys of everlasting sweetness.[11]

There is an organic progression for these steps. The first rung we step on is reading Scripture (*lectio*) in a careful and focused manner. As one reads a particular passage of Scripture, key words, themes, or ideas come to mind. Following *lectio* is meditation (*meditatio*), which is a thorough reflecting on what emerged during reading. This meditation provides the language, vocabulary, and subject matter for conversing with God. Meditation leads to the dialogue of prayer (*oratio*) where one expresses how the matter of mediation moves one's heart. Finally, prayer can dispose us to the gift of contemplation (*contemplatio*), which is the experience of God marked by joy and peace.

When I first read Guigo's description of *lectio divina* and the ordering of the various rungs or steps, several things not only surprised me, but also opened my eyes to obstacles that had hindered my own prayer life. First, I was surprised to find "prayer" designated as just

---

[11]   Guigo, *A Ladder of Monks and Twelve Meditations*, p. 68.

one of the four steps. In this Guigo echoes the Fathers of the Church, who teach that we hear God when we read Scripture (*lectio*), but we talk to him when we pray (*oratio*). Thus, prayer, technically speaking, is where we talk to God by expressing our thoughts and feelings. What was surprising for me was that this was the third step, for I had often thought of prayer as the starting place.

Additionally, Guigo described contemplation (*contemplatio*), which is a pure gift in which our hearts are taken up in a loving gaze of God, as the *final* step. We often come to prayer looking for contemplation, but we begin without the divine dialogue that leads to contemplation. In doing so, we immediately reach for the third and fourth rungs of Guigo's ladder. Unfortunately, our straining for the these higher rungs often makes prayer an exercise in frustration, as we can't reach them without a foothold to assist our ascent. Instead of starting at the first or second rung, we want to skip ahead to the latter stages of prayer, and thus find what we are striving for out of reach. I think this explains why so many people find prayer so difficult. It only takes a few such failed attempts and we quickly surmise that prayer and contemplation are not for us.

When a child is learning to climb stairs for the first time, we teach them to take one careful step at a time. And they do this for quite some time, until their little legs grow in size and strength. But later, as they grow and become more agile, they may skip steps and ascend the staircase at a faster pace. But even as an adult, more often than not, the staircase is ascended one step at a time. Our prayer is like this. While God can lead our heart at times directly to *oratio* or *contemplatio*, most often it will prove fruitful to ascend one rung at a time. Even great saints like St. Teresa of Avila did not seek to enter immediately into contemplation, but approached prayer by making use of Scripture and books for meditation.

Such false expectations of instant prayer and contemplation, along with the assumption that they will come without much effort, may be the biggest obstacle to achieving a regular and fruitful prayer life. Upon reflection, the absurdity of such a notion is obvious. It is like someone thinking they could purchase a vineyard in the springtime and come back six months later to find bottled wine. We shouldn't waltz into a chapel and expect instant contemplation any more than you would expect to walk into a vineyard and out the other side with a fine Cabernet Sauvignon. And yet, for some strange reason, we envision that we should be able to taste the rich fruits of contemplation without working in the vineyard of Sacred Scripture.

Working the Vineyard

I have friends who own a vineyard in Virginia. I have visited it repeatedly and watched how the vines grow and take shape to fill out the trellises. I have seen the effort put into tilling the earth, planting the vines, fertilizing, watering, nurturing, and dressing the growing plants, and tending the grapes during the growing period. I have walked through the wine cellar and smelled the enormous and handsome oak barrels that hold the liquid treasure.

When I first met my friends, they had just started their vineyard. One of the primary grapes they planted was the Norton, which many consider the only true (quality) red table wine grape that is native to America. It is a wonderful wine, with a dark purple color and a firm but velvety texture that puts forth a penetrating aroma and flavor. I thought the idea of a vineyard in Virginia rather novel until I learned about the Old Dominion's wine history. In 1830, Dr. Norton, from Richmond, began to market "the Norton," a great red wine with many virtues. The Norton grape grows vigorously, is one of the most disease-resistant varieties, and has almost twice as much *reservatrol* (the chemical in red wine that confers so many health benefits) as any other wine. The Norton was instantly a commercial success. Before the Civil War, Virginia, with its Norton grape, was the hub of American winemaking. But by the end of the war, almost all of Virginia's vineyards were destroyed and its economy was in shambles, and California, now connected by rail with the East, quickly became the major supplier of domestic wine. Only in recent years is the Norton once again making a comeback with new vineyards all over Virginia.

So, it was with fascination that I watched my friends establish their vineyard. On the one hand, it is hard work starting a new vineyard, work that really takes years to pay off. On the other hand, God does all the *really* hard work of providing the sunshine, soil, and rain, and creating and sustaining the chemical processes that take place in each and every cell of the grapevine. Indeed, winemaking is one of those great arts in which man learns to work with the amazing gifts of creation.

The spiritual life is a bit like this. On the one hand, God needs nothing from us. He not only invented the universe without us, He invented *us* without us. Everything we have is a gift, including our very existence. Our ability to will, to work, to please God, to desire what is good, are all gifts from God that we merely give back to Him. That is why Jesus says, in a context in which He is speaking about vines, "You did not choose me, but I chose you and appointed you that you should go and bear fruit and that your fruit should abide" (Jn 15:16). The same God who makes the vineyard fruitful, makes us fruitful too.

On the other hand, as St. Augustine says, "God created us without us: but he did not will to save us without us."[12] Following St. Paul, Augustine understood that salvation is the free gift of God, which means not only that we cannot earn it (otherwise it wouldn't be a gift) but also that it really is *ours* (because God really gives it to us). Yet it is our responsibility to avail ourselves of that gift and "work out our salvation with fear and trembling" (Phil 2:12). We have to cooperate with God's grace as best we can. God has given us all the resources we need. Now it is our task to cultivate the soil and care for the vine He has planted so that we bear the fruit He desires.

Such cultivation takes work, regardless of whether it is producing fine wine, holiness, or intimate prayer. The saints did not start out as experts in prayer but had to work at it, just as a great musician must work at his craft. Many think that Mozart was simply gifted with a prodigious talent for writing symphonies. Nothing could be further from the truth, as Mozart himself wrote to a friend: "People err who think my art comes easily to me. I assure you, dear friend, nobody has devoted so much time and thought to composition as I. There is not a famous master whose music I have not industriously studied through many times."[13] Mozart was by no means exaggerating; his hand was crippled by the time he was twenty-eight years old from all the practices and performances and from gripping a quill pen to write and rewrite his music. Mozart became a great musician, like the saints

---

[12] St. Augustine, *Sermo* 169, 11, 13: PL 38, 923

[13] As quoted in Twyla Tharp's, *The Creative Habit: Learn it and Use it for Life* (New York: Simon & Schuster, 2005), p. 5.

became great friends of God, through the arduous effort that can be sustained only by love for what one pursues.

In the Vineyard of the Text

The process of prayer is strikingly similar to cultivating wine. The hard work of preparing the soil and planting the vines, is analogous to the equally arduous effort of breaking up the hard ground of our heart and planting the seeds of the Gospel. And the fruit that grows must be collected in the well-known stages of harvest.

At harvest time in the vineyard you first walk through the rows of vines and pick the grapes. Picking grapes is tedious and time consuming, done by hand so as not to damage the grapes. So too, the first rung of prayer, the reading (*lectio*) of Scripture, must be done with care and concentration. Readers must make their way carefully through the lines of the text, selecting key words and phrases that stand out to them.

After the grapes are picked, they are put in a large vat, and if you have friends who have a vineyard you may even get to take your shoes off, roll up your pants, and tread on the grapes! The juice must be squeezed out. Similarly, in the second rung of meditation, *meditatio*, we squeeze out the meaning of the text we have carefully read in *lectio*. Once the juices are collected they are given time for fermentation. This is like prayer (*oratio*), where the heart ponders and reflects on what the mind has meditated, and its feelings bubble up to a heartfelt transformation and dialogue with God.

The last and final stage is the finest. After the wine has had time to ferment, age, and find its balance, under the guidance of the expert vintner, one gets to taste the fine wine. It is striking how the biblical tradition describes contemplation (*contemplatio*) as something to be "tasted" and "savored." This is expressed often in the Psalms, which call us to "taste and see the goodness of the Lord" (Ps 34:8).

Here is a simple outline to help visualize these vital steps to harvesting the vineyard of the divine text, a summary of the rungs of Guigo's ladder of *lectio divina*:

Lectio	In which the words of Scripture are examined closely, their connections and patterns noted. Similar to how the grapes of a vineyard are examined and collected with care.
Meditatio	In which this reading of Scripture is squeezed to extract its meaning. Similar to how grapes are squeezed for their juice.
Oratio	In which our conversation with God about the Word allows us to ponder it in our heart with a growing desire for the One who has spoken to us. Similar to how grape juice ferments over time in an oak barrel to produce the sweet wine.
Contemplatio	In which we "taste the goodness of the Lord." Similar to how the wine is opened and its sweetness consumed.
	Following these four steps, and in response to them, we can add a fifth step:
Operatio	In which we make operative some practical resolution to bring the wine of God's Word to fruitfulness in our life and the world.

The monks who relished the idea of Scripture being a spiritual vineyard surely grasped just how analogous winemaking is to *lectio divina*. Perhaps this is why so many monasteries specialized in making wine. The monks found that *lectio divina*, like winemaking, was always worth the effort.

Taste and See

Some might say, "*Lectio divina* was invented by and for monks. Can it really be practiced by ordinary people living busy lives?" The answer to such a question is given by Pope Benedict XVI. Since the start of his pontificate in April 2005, Pope Benedict has strongly championed the use of *lectio divina* for everybody. Like Christ on the road to Emmaus, Pope Benedict's first two synods emphasized Eucharist and Scripture—word and sacrament—as the keys to the New Evangelization. On September 16, 2005, the fortieth anniversary of *Dei Verbum*, the Second Vatican Council's great document on Scripture, Pope Benedict said: "If [*lectio divina*] is effectively promoted, this practice will bring to the Church—I am convinced—a new spiritual springtime."

In those words, the Holy Father is echoing Vatican II:

> The Church forcefully and specially exhorts all the Christian faithful … to learn the surpassing knowledge of Jesus Christ (Phil 3:8) by frequent reading of the divine Scriptures … Let them remember, however, that prayer should accompany the reading of Sacred Scripture, so that a dialogue takes place between God and man.[14]

---

[14] *Dei Verbum* 25; *Catechism of the Catholic Church*, 2653

And the Council is simply echoing Catholic teaching that stretches back to the greatest biblical scholar of antiquity, St. Jerome:

> The Lord's flesh is real food and his blood real drink; this is our true good in this present life: to nourish ourselves with his flesh and to drink his blood in not only the Eucharist but also the reading of Sacred Scriptures, is real food and real drink.[15]

If we are to know Christ more and experience the eagerly awaited spiritual springtime, we will need to be nourished by the Scriptures, and what better way than by practicing the ancient method of *lectio divina*.

Jesus once remarked to His disciples, "I sent you to reap that for which you did not labor; others have labored, and you have entered into their labor" (Jn 4:38). What did He mean? Think about the time Jesus changed the water to wine at Cana. The steward of the feast remarked, "Every man serves the good wine first; and when men have drunk freely, then the poor wine; but you have kept the good wine until now" (Jn 2:10). John records that remark because it has a double meaning for the Church. The "best wine" is the Eucharistic wine of the New Covenant. Instead of pouring it out on Abraham, Moses, and the prophets, God chose to make it a gift in "the fullness of time": the last days, which were inaugurated by Christ's Passion and Resurrection. As the letter to the Hebrews puts it, "[A]ll these, though well attested by their faith, did not receive what was promised, since God had foreseen something better for us, that apart from us they should not be made perfect" (Heb 11:39-40).

This New Testament pattern of "saving the best for last" is still

---

[15] St. Jerome, *Commentarius in Ecclesiasten*, 313: CCL 72, 278

true today. As medieval scholars pointed out, we see further than our ancestors because we "stand on the shoulders of giants." Therefore, what the monks brought to birth with great labor over many centuries is given to us freely by Mother Church so that the gifts of God may be multiplied and the Church can grow in unity not only across the world but down through the ages.

Thus, Pope John Paul II addresses the following words to *all* of us:

> It is especially necessary that listening to the Word of God should become a life-giving encounter, in the ancient and ever valid tradition of *lectio divina*, which draws from the biblical text the living word which questions, directs and shapes our lives.[16]

Pope John Paul II's passionate call to practice *lectio divina* is made in his heartfelt letter to the universal Church issued at the end of the Jubilee year in 2000. This letter is a beautiful summary of the fruits of the holy year and was presented by John Paul II as a spiritual blueprint for the new springtime for the Church and the world that he hoped would emerge in the new millennium. In other words, *lectio divina* is an integral part of the Church's game plan for the renewal of faith in our times.

The Way Up

For a new springtime to emerge in our own prayer life, in the life of the Church, and in the world around us, however, we will have to cooperate with the work the master vintner desires to do in our lives. If we are going to climb the ladder of *lectio divina,* this will mean work, something will be required of us. Nobody climbs a ladder without

16 John Paul II, *Novo Millennio Ineunte* (6 January 2001), 39: AAS 93 (2001), 293.

effort, and nobody climbs a ladder to heaven without sustained effort. It is not necessary to have a doctorate in Scripture or know Greek or Latin to practice *lectio divina*, but neither is it for the lazy. One needs to be willing to exercise some self-discipline, to make the time and interior space necessary to really focus on a deep reading and learning of the Word of God.

We cannot keep this potent method bottled up and stored in the ancient wine cellars of the Church's traditions. It is time to uncork the power of prayer in our daily lives, so that we can "taste and see the goodness of the Lord" (Ps 34:8). The best place to start is the first rung of Guigo's ladder to heaven, *lectio*, and so we now turn to the art of reading Scripture well. As the Spirit said to St. Augustine, so He says to us: "Take and read."

Chapter Three

Lectio

Your word is a lamp to my feet and a light to my path.
— Psalm 119:105

In the sacred books, the Father who is in heaven comes lovingly to meet his children, and talks with them.
— Dei Verbum, 21

The Sacred Page

A generation ago, if someone in Denver told you that they had spent the day surfing, you might have considered committing them to an institution. Today, if someone said that, at worst you would chide them for wasting too much time. It is an ancient feature of linguistic development for a culture to apply pre-existent terms to new items of technology. A term once used to describe skimming the surface of a broad body of water is now also used to describe gliding seamlessly over vast oceans of information stored on the World Wide Web. Indeed, the word "web" itself now encompasses a reality far surpassing anything Charlotte or her kin could ever have spun.

Like pouring new wine into old wineskins, old words often acquire new meanings and nuances. Such a thing also happened in Roman antiquity when a new-fangled invention called the "codex" or "book" began to appear. It was less cumbersome than the scroll, and more conducive for finding information and cross-referencing ideas (because you could navigate more quickly through pages rather than laboriously rolling and unrolling a scroll). Therefore, it eventually replaced the scroll as a means of transmitting the written word.

Within the Christian community, as might be expected, the codex soon became the medium of choice for preserving the text of Scripture and other sacred writings. The Benedictine monks were on the cutting edge of this new technology, studiously copying God's Word, as well as texts both sacred and secular into books that were preserved in their monasteries. This important work (*labora*) was added to their prayer (*ora*) and other monastic duties. The joining of this task with their labor in the fields produced an unexpected correlation. The monks noticed that the squared leaves of vellum that were bound together to form a codex looked curiously similar to the wooden trellises that ensured fruitful growth in their vineyards and gardens. These sturdy, square lattices constructed for the vines were called *paginae*. It wasn't long before the monks dubbed the square leaves of Scripture *sacrae paginae* ("sacred pages"). Some believe that the etymology for the Latin word *pagina*, from which we get the English word "page," can be traced to the square trellis used in the vineyard.[17]

The monks elaborated on this theme, decorating the manuscripts themselves. The pages of Scripture were painted with vines along the margins. Great bunches of grapes were hung from the elaborate, aggrandized capital letters. Such decoration communicated the

---

[17] On the origins of the term *sacra pagina*, see Ivan Illich, *In the Vineyard of the Text: A Commentary to Hugh's Didascalicon* (Chicago: University of Chicago Press, 1993), pp. 57-58.

monastic understanding that their life included not only laboring in the *paginae* of the vineyard to bring forth grapes for wine, but also laboring in the *paginae* of Scripture to bring forth the fine wine of God's revelation. Besides the vineyard of the field there was the sacred vineyard of the Word. This explains why *sacra pagina* was a favorite term in the Middle Ages for Sacred Scripture.

Read and Re-Read

Such laboring in the sacred page is exactly what is called for in the *lectio* step when practicing *lectio divina*. If we want to hear God in our prayer, the first step is reading well. But intelligent reading comes only with practice. And in an age of cable, Internet, and video-on-demand that discourages reading in favor of the visual, reading has become a lost art. Sadly, very few experience the joys of being "lost" in a book, whether it is well-written fiction or a thoughtful treatise on a subject of interest. When we do read, our culture constantly exhorts us to "cut to the chase" and just "get the gist" of what we read. Airports are filled with "disposable" books that are meant to be read during a single flight and flung aside. Magazine articles highlight the key ideas in bold print in side boxes on each page. And many high school and college students often opt to skim Cliff Notes rather than labor through a lengthy novel.

In contrast, the first thing *lectio* calls us to do is *slow down*. As the twelfth-century Cistercian monk William of St. Thierry puts it: "In all Scripture, diligent reading is as far from superficial perusal as friendship is distinct from acquaintance with a stranger, or as affection given to a companion differs from a casual greeting."[18]

---

[18] William of St. Thierry, *The Golden Epistle*, #121; SChr 223, p. 238.

As you begin *lectio*, then, take a moment to ask God to help you switch off the cell phone in your soul. Let your pulse slow down a bit. Get off the mental treadmill and reduce your pace from breathless sprint to that of a stroll in the vineyard. Instead of reading a book in order to get to the end and dispose of it like a candy bar wrapper, we are going to imitate the monks of old and ruminate on the text.

It was commonplace for medieval monks to read the same book over and over again throughout their lives. Just as a gardener regularly turns over the soil, they would deepen their familiarity with the language and style of a particular book, allowing the words to soak into their minds and hearts, watering their spiritual lives. This practice of re-reading was applied to Scripture as well. For the monks, reading the word of Scripture, like tending an expansive vineyard, was a lifelong task. Pope Benedict XVI has remarked that *lectio divina* "consists in pouring over a biblical text for some time, reading it and rereading it, as it were, 'ruminating' on it as the Fathers say and squeezing from it, so to speak, all its 'juice,' so that it may nourish meditation and contemplation and like water, succeed in irrigating life itself."[19] Scripture is life-giving, but we must labor in the vineyard of the text with care if our reading of Scripture is to be fruitful.

Strategies for Reading

In order to help increase the fruitfulness of your own labors in the *sacra pagina*, we will now look at several "trellises"—examples that illustrate strategies essential for reading Scripture well. These are

---

[19] Benedict XVI, *Angelus Message*, 6 November 2005.

some of the basic tips I teach my students to equip them to become good readers of Scripture.

Let's start with the simple, as the essential is often what is simplest. Like any good journalist, when we come to a text we need to ask ourselves the four basic questions: who, what, when and where. One helpful way of answering these questions is to pay close attention to the basic building blocks of grammar. We should ask ourselves "What nouns and verbs are used in the passage? Who and what is this passage about? What action is happening? Where is the event we are reading about taking place, and what other events in Scripture took place here as well?" As simple as such questions may seem, they can pay rich dividends in beginning our dialogue with God. Good reading must take the time to grapple with these basic questions if we are ever going to penetrate the surface of the text.

Details

As we begin to answer these basic questions, we encounter the first necessary and vital strategy for good *lectio*: recognizing details. Reading Scripture requires a keen eye to discern the author's often-subtle artistry. Before the invention of the printing press and the wide distribution of books, each scroll or codex was hand-written and often beautifully illustrated, making such works extremely expensive and difficult to produce. As a result, what was written was done with forethought and care. If an author decided to take time and space to note an extra detail or repeat a word or idea, it behooves us to pay close attention. Every word is important.

In stark contrast is the often extravagant and superfluous use of words and detail in modern writing. With paper costing two cents a page we can afford to dole out words and descriptions with abandon. A character's face can be described in more detail and words than Scripture uses for the creation of the world in Genesis 1. Word inflation numbs us to the subtle yet striking skill that ancient authors employed with the smallest details. Such detail in Scripture matters. For example, we are well into the Joseph story before we are told that he is "handsome and good looking" (Gn 39:6). It is no superfluous detail. Early on in the story, when Joseph was with his brothers, his good looks did not matter. It is not until he is alone with Potipher's wife that Joseph's attractiveness matters in the story's plot.

St. John also uses such detail in the final chapter of his gospel when he notes that Jesus asked Peter three times, "Do you love me?" (Jn 21:9-19). An often overlooked detail in the narrative is that this thrice-repeated question is asked near the "charcoal fire" on which Jesus had prepared a breakfast meal for His disciples. An attentive reader will recall that the only other time John's gospel records the presence of a charcoal fire is when Peter stood beside a charcoal fire warming himself and denied Jesus three times (Jn 18:17-18). The repetition of the charcoal fire links these two passages, allowing us to see how Peter's threefold confession of love atones for his threefold denial. A single detail in Scripture can often communicate more than page full of words in a modern book.

The ancient craft of writing did not highlight for the reader why certain details mattered; it was up to the reader to make the connection. For example, when the author of 1 Samuel takes time to note that Saul was "taller than any of the people" (1 Sam 9:2), it seems to be an aside with little importance. However, several chapters later in 1 Samuel 17 when a giant of a man comes onto the battlefield at a height of "six cubits and a span" (1 Sam 17:4), the author's detail about Saul makes it clear that he was the best suited warrior in all of Israel to go up against Goliath. Surely, the largest Israelite should fight the Philistine giant. Instead, David, whom Samuel anointed only after God told him to bypass David's brothers and not to judge based on the "height of his stature," will be the one to defeat Goliath, overcoming his lack of stature with his trust in God as his deliverer.

Later, among David's own sons, one cannot appreciate the significance of Absalom's demise if the details of his detention in a tree are not connected to a much earlier detail of the narrative. After his army's defeat, Absalom rides his mule in an attempt to flee, but he is caught up when his hair becomes entangled in the branches of an oak tree (2 Sam 18:9). This may seem a rather odd way for Absalom to be hung out to dry, but the discerning reader remembers that earlier in the story Absalom's vain pride in his hair and good looks was highlighted when the narrator described how Absalom cut his hair only once a year and then took the time to weigh it, with it coming in at the notable amount of 200 shekels weight! Absalom's undoing was not a freak accident, rather the narrative details make it clear that Absalom's vanity led to his undoing.

As Albert Einstein once observed, God is in the details. If that is true of the book of creation, how much more is it true of the inspired book of Scripture.

Repetition

Once we learn to look for details in the text, we are better prepared to discern patterns of repetition also. For example, in the creation story we hear that for every day "there was evening" and thus an ending; each day, that is, but the last. The seventh day has no ending, and that is very important in the author's creation poem, as the seventh day, the Sabbath, is a hint of the eternal rest of heaven that will have no end. In Genesis 3, the subtle serpent promises Eve that if she eats the forbidden fruit she will become "like" God. The enemy is repeating the precious word "like" that was used by God Himself as a description of the nature of made man and woman, who were created in God's own image and "likeness" (Gn 1:26). The repetition communicates a profoundly ironic point, the woman grasps for the fruit in order to obtain what had already been given to her. If we don't observe carefully the patterns of repetition woven into the biblical narratives, our reading will likewise be a grasping for something we just don't understand.

Repetition can also serve to reinforce the author's primary point. Thus, the author of Psalm 121 repeatedly refers to God as the one who will "keep" or protect. Six times God is described as the one who keeps, which in Hebrew is the verb *shamir*, a word that implies protection and care. Like a drumbeat, the psalmist tells those who are in search of security to put their trust in the Lord. All parents, who often have to repeat soothing words to the anxious hearts of their children, understand well this pedagogy of repetition.

I could keep compiling examples of repetition, but by now you should grasp the importance of this simple yet often sophisticated method of the ancient authors. It is not without reason that one of the classic proverbs of education is: *Repetitio est mater studiorum*, "repetition is the mother of all learning." I find that when I teach, I can't say that enough to my students.

Allusion

Without a keen eye for detail we will, more often than not, miss the amazing patterns of repetition hidden throughout the biblical texts. What is more, the smallest details betray patterns of repetition that are often meant to allude to earlier stories and events. So, for example, in the story of Noah, when the waters part and the dry ground appears, we are reminded of how the same language was used to describe the events on the third day of creation. With the flood waters receded, God blesses Noah and commands him and his children to be fruitful and multiply. Noah, in other words, is a new Adam in the midst of a new creation. Unfortunately for Noah, his parallels with Adam continue. He builds a garden-like vineyard, imbibes too much of its fruit and ends up naked and ashamed: a new fall follows hard upon this new creation. The rest of biblical history will revel in this allusive story-telling technique. If we have ears to hear we will catch all kinds of allusions.

Sometimes finding that vitally important detail can be like locating the proverbial needle in a haystack, especially for those of us not accustomed to reading well. But once having found it, it can thread together two very different stories from different times. I found this to be true when writing an article entitled "Holy Night, Silent Knight" about St. Joseph's role in the infancy narratives of Matthew's gospel. Writing the article necessitated a careful reading and rereading of Matthew's story of St. Joseph in his opening chapters. As I read, a detail I had never before noticed leapt out at me: it was the name of Joseph's father, Jacob (Mt 1:15-16). When a Jewish man named Jacob names his son Joseph, a biblically literate reader would immediately recall the classic story in Genesis of Jacob and his favorite son, Joseph.

I had been so numbed by the long genealogy in Matthew that by the time I reached the end I never noticed the significance of the name of St. Joseph's father.

This inconspicuous detail makes for a very quiet echo to the story of the Old Testament Joseph, but if we are not listening for details given at the level of a whisper we will walk on by. The allusive whisper to Joseph's story in the Old Testament echoes ever louder as we make our way through Mathew's opening chapters. Matthew tells us that Joseph, a just man, receives angelic messages in his dreams. When we hear of the divine communication to Joseph through dreams we would have to be biblically tone-deaf not to notice the echoes reverberating from the Old Testament story of a Joseph who kept having dreams, especially since both dreaming Josephs end up in the same place, Egypt. The Old Testament Joseph is able to save the lives of Jacob's twelve sons in Egypt, while Mary's Joseph spares the one who will save all of Israel, Jesus.

All these allusions invite us to make further connections. The Old Testament Joseph's refusal to sleep with his master's wife anticipates the same heroic chastity in the later Joseph who protects the Virgin Mother of the Messiah. Only by noting the pattern of detail can we see how the allusive power of the story weaves together the old with the new, and the final product is a rich interwoven tapestry of many colors. Indeed, it is because of our love for these biblical stories about these two holy men that my wife and I named our son Joseph. Scripture's story has ways of spilling out from the confines of the text and into our present, if we just take up the story and read.

It is not just ancient Hebrew culture that uses such methods, for we make use of allusion all the time. A friend of mine has a son named Luke, and sometimes when he is joking around he will say, in a deep, ominous voice, "Luke! I am your father!" Everyone gets the joke without my friend having to laboriously explain that he is quoting a line from *Star Wars*. That's allusion. When Dwight Eisenhower entitled his memoirs of World War II *Crusade in Europe*, he was alluding to the image of the valiant Christian knight at war with the forces of evil. When George Bush made the allusion to the Crusades after September 11th he failed to realize how such a potent image would be received by the Muslim world. His words reverberated throughout the Middle East and evoked a far different version of the Crusades than the one Eisenhower and the West told. Echoes and allusions have profound power because they evoke stories, and stories grab hold of our imagination and touch the deepest part of our hearts and minds.

With a simple passing reference to an image, song, story, speech, or other aspect of our culture and history, it is possible to communicate truth, move hearts, and inspire great deeds. Scripture makes use of allusion constantly, and the authors expect us to "hear" the allusions they are making. All of this means we need to know the story of Scripture better than we know the story of *Star Wars*. This is one of the reasons that a constant reading of Scripture pays off. You begin to catch the subtle play of ideas and references that the biblical authors are making in their symphonic conversation with one another. In reading Scripture, we enter into a long conversation between the various inspired authors, symphonically conducted by the Holy Spirit. It's almost like a fugue in music, where certain ideas and themes will sound and play off one another in new and unexpected combinations so that new depths of meaning are revealed. Reading Scripture well takes time, but, much like a fine wine, its taste only gets better.

An Example of Lectio

With our heightened awareness of how to read Scripture well, let's take a look at Psalm 1 and focus on the first stage of *lectio divina*, namely *lectio* or reading. Begin by reading and then re-reading the psalm:

> Blessed is the man who walks not in the counsel of the wicked,
> Nor stands in the way of sinners, nor sits in the seat of scoffers;
> But his delight is in the law of the LORD, and on his law he meditates day and night.
> He is like a tree planted by streams of water, that yields its fruit in its season,
> And its leaf does not wither. In all that he does, he prospers.
> The wicked are not so, but are like chaff which the wind drives away.
> Therefore the wicked will not stand in the judgment,
> Nor sinners in the congregation of the righteous;
> For the LORD knows the way of the righteous,
> But the way of the wicked will perish.

We begin, as noted above, by asking questions (*Who? What? When? Where?*) and looking for details. In Psalm 1 we have a righteous man and a wicked man. There is the action of walking, standing and sitting. There is the image of a tree, its action of being planted, yielding fruit and not withering. There is the image of chaff, wind and judgment. This list isn't exhaustive, but it will get us started.

When we look at how these nouns and verbs are used, we quickly notice a pattern in Psalm 1's use of triple emphases. This is particularly important in the Old Testament because Hebrew does not, like English, employ superlatives. It has no words to express comparisons between "good, better, supremely good, or best." Instead, emphasis is achieved by repetition. So, for instance, the cherubim in Isaiah 6:3 cry "Holy, Holy, Holy!" in praise of God: the Hebrew way of saying God is Supremely Holy, the most holy.

Additionally, Hebrew poetry does not rely on rhyming *sounds*, but on rhyming *ideas* for its power. Psalms (including this one) will say the same thing different ways ("Blessed is the man/who *walks not in the counsel of the wicked,*/nor *stands in the way of sinners,*/ nor *sits in the seat of scoffers*"). This way of rhyming ideas gives an image a kind of cumulative power, but also allows us to explore what is being said from different angles. The triple emphases of Psalm 1 shows us a progression in sin. The wicked man walks, then stands, and finally sits. His moral life follows a progression from walking toward temptation, to standing and lingering in his sinful choice, to sitting down—immobilized by the consequences of sin in his life.

Jesus uses the same technique when He says "ask, and it will be given you; seek, and you will find; knock, and it will be opened to you" (Mt 7:7). Jesus' saying gives us an image of prayer that moves from mere passivity ("ask") to activity ("seek") to an insistent and even importunate kind of prayer ("knock"). As we familiarize ourselves more with Jesus' teaching on prayer, we discover that, far from urging us to offer milk-and-water prayers, Jesus actually commends prayer that bangs on God's door and won't let Him rest until it is answered (Lk 18:1-8).

Image is Everything

In 1990, the camera giant Canon launched one of the most successful ad campaigns in modern marketing. The charismatic tennis player Andre Agassi pronounced its home-run marketing motto, "Image is everything." Juxtaposing scenes of Agassi taking shots with a Canon camera on a tennis court with clips of his lightning-fast tennis swings made a hit with the public and left an indelible image on the consumer mind. We all know that a picture is worth a thousand words, and the mark of a masterful author is the ability to paint a picture in a reader's mind. Long before the invention of cameras, the authors of Scripture, many whom were masterful communicators, understood the profound power of images. The tapestry of Scripture is a collection of masterful word pictures woven throughout the fabric of biblical speech. Therefore, it is important to pay attention to the concrete imagery the Scriptural writers use.

Biblical writers are profoundly concrete thinkers, particularly in comparison to modern writers. George Orwell famously demonstrated this when he quoted a well-known verse from Ecclesiastes 9:11:

> I returned and saw under the sun, that the race is not to the swift, nor the battle to the strong, neither yet bread to the wise, nor yet riches to men of understanding, nor yet favour to men of skill; but time and chance happeneth to all of them.

Then Orwell re-wrote the verse in deadly modern bureaucratic prose:

> Objective consideration of contemporary phenomena compels the conclusion that success or failure in competitive activities exhibits no tendency to be commen-

surate with innate capacity, but that a considerable element of the unpredictable must invariably be taken into account.[20]

No image is accidental in the biblical texts, they all demand our attention. Use all your senses in reading, just as the ancient writers used all their senses in writing. Note, for instance, that the psalmist does not say that the blessed man "always" meditates on the law of the Lord. You can't picture "always." But you can picture "day and night." Call these images to mind as you read them, noting what they are trying to communicate and also noting other locations in Scripture where these images have been used.

The reason why this is important is because, as Mark Twain said, "History doesn't repeat itself, but it rhymes." God does something in the history of revelation very much like what the Hebrew writers do in rhyming ideas and images throughout the history of Israel. Themes and images occur and recur, building in power and meaning as revelation progresses.

As we place the psalm in the context of the rest of Scripture, we discover a wealth of other connections. For example, the image of the tree and the waters is an image that stretches back to the world's very beginning. In Genesis 1 and 2, after the emergence of the world out of "the deep," Eden is described as a garden watered by four rivers. In it was the "tree of life," as well as the tree of the knowledge of good and evil. The waters again appear in Genesis 6-9 in the story of Noah and the first sign of life is from the branch of an olive tree. In Exodus, Moses purified water in the wilderness by throwing a tree into the

---

[20] George Orwell, "Politics and the English Language," *The New Republic*, June 17-24, 1946.

waters, which makes them sweet to drink (Ex 15:23-25). After the destruction of the Temple, Ezekiel has a vision in which he sees a restored Temple with a river flowing out of it with trees planted beside it (Ez 47:1-12).

Again, in the description of the righteous in Psalm 92:12-15, we see the curious juxtaposition of trees that never wither with the Temple: "The righteous flourish like the palm tree, and grow like a cedar in Lebanon. They are planted in the house of the LORD, they flourish in the courts of our God. They still bring forth fruit in old age, they are ever full of sap and green, to show that the LORD is upright."

Jesus, standing before the Temple centuries later, will tell us that He is the true Temple (Jn 2:19) and that whoever believes in Him will have rivers of living water flowing out of his heart (Jn 7:38). In fact, the gospel of John is framed by images of water, from Jesus' baptism in the Jordan to the flow of blood and water while he hung on a "tree." This moment during Jesus' death is so important that John departs from his narrative description of the crucifixion to remind us that he was an eyewitness of the event (Jn 19:34-35).

When Paul meditates on the relationship of Gentiles to Jews in Romans 9-11, he compares those who are faithful to God to an olive tree, much like the blessed man in Psalm 52:8: "But I am like a green olive tree in the house of God."

Finally, John will see a vision of the New Jerusalem in which Ezekiel's images are recovered in the apostle's glorious vision of "the river of the water of life, bright as crystal, flowing from the throne of God and of the Lamb through the middle of the street of the city; also, on either side of the river, the tree of life with its twelve kinds of fruit, yielding its fruit each month; and the leaves of the tree were for the healing of the nations" (Rv 22:1-2). In this New Jerusalem, there is no Temple because "its temple is the Lord God the Almighty and the Lamb" (Rv 21:22).

Such careful reading and rereading of Scripture produces a bountiful harvest of a great many "grapes" from Scripture, along with the realization that there are a myriad of connections between the deceptively simple images of a tree and the waters of life. And because Jesus assures us that it is so, you can likewise be confident that these images are not mere happenstance, but are given by the Holy Spirit to teach us about Christ (Lk 24:44–45).

But to do that, the grapes must be squeezed to extract their juice. And that is the work of the next phase of *lectio divina: meditatio.*

Chapter Four

Meditatio

It is the glory of God to conceal things, but the glory of kings is to search things out.
— Proverbs 25:2

Reading is like a first foundation; it gives us matter for meditation.
Meditation seeks more diligently what is to be sought. It is like the
digging that finds a treasure (Proverbs 2:4; Mt 13:44) and so
we are led to prayer . . . Reading, as it were, puts the solid food
into our mouths, meditation chews it and breaks it down.
— Guigo the Carthusian

Meditation has fallen on hard times these days. If asked to describe what comes to mind when we hear the term "meditation," many of us would describe esoteric images and ideas, such as the breathing techniques and sitting positions found in yoga. Some think of mediation as an attempt to get outside and beyond the "thinking mind" and into a state of relaxation or consciousness which allows the mind essentially to be "emptied" in order to become aware of something deeper. Often this "something deeper" is nothing more than our emotions and feelings, and it is often quite far from the original transcendent experience sought.

Such a shallow understanding of meditation is all too common nowadays. A quick internet search of the word "meditation" or reading its Wikipedia entry will reveal that the Christian sense of the word is largely lost. While the ancient Eastern methods of meditation have a certain rigor of body and mind, they lack the substance and true end of classical Christian meditation. God created the human person, mind, body, and soul, giving us a free will and a rational intellect. The will was made to love and the mind to think. But the goal of much modern meditation is simply relaxation and or self-awareness gained by emptying the mind. An empty mind, however, is like an empty gas tank or an empty stomach; either way, you can't get far on empty.

In the gospels, Jesus reminds us that the "mind" is a very important part of our relationship with God. In fact, Jesus does a remarkable thing in His teaching to emphasize the importance of the mind. In Deuteronomy 6:4-5, God gives Israel the great creedal summary of all Israelite belief and practice, known as the *Shema*: "Hear, O Israel: The LORD our God is one LORD; and you shall love the LORD your God with all your heart, and with all your soul, and with all your might."

However, when Jesus quotes the *Shema* in Mark 12:28-30, He actually adds an important clause:

> And one of the scribes came up and heard them disputing with one another, and seeing that he answered them well, asked him, "Which commandment is the first of all?" Jesus answered, "The first is, 'Hear, O Israel: The LORD our God, the LORD is one; and you shall love the LORD your God with all your heart, and with all your soul, *and with all your mind*, and with all your strength'" (emphasis added).

Why does Jesus offer this "inspired" addition? Because our minds are given to us to be used, not wiped clean, bypassed, or ignored. We need to "open our minds" not to empty them out, but rather to fill them with knowledge and understanding and truth. In the words of G.K. Chesterton, "The object of opening the mind, as of opening the mouth, is to shut it again on something solid."[21]

St. Paul, like his Master, emphasizes the great importance of the mind repeatedly throughout his letters. Paul warns that one of the marks of the Fall is that humans often set aside their reason and allow their lives to be governed by their passions:

> Ever since the creation of the world his invisible nature, namely, his eternal power and deity, has been clearly perceived in the things that have been made. So they are without excuse; for although they knew God they did not honor him as God or give thanks to him, but they became futile in their thinking and their senseless minds were darkened (Rom 1:20-21).

Or again, as he warned the Ephesians:

> Now this I affirm and testify in the Lord, that you must no longer live as the Gentiles do, in the futility of their minds; they are darkened in their understanding, alienated from the life of God because of the ignorance that is in them, due to their hardness of heart (Eph 4:17-18).

For Paul, one of the primary casualties of sin is the "darkening" of the mind. Sin corrupts the will and disorders our desires, but what we often forget is that it also dims our understanding and blinds us to the things of God, besides dulling our common sense.

St. Paul not only speaks of the consequences of sin, he also makes clear that one of the fruits (and responsibilities) of a life renewed by

---

[21] G. K. Chesterton, *The Collected Works of G. K. Chesterton Vol. 16: The Autobiography* (San Francisco: Ignatius, 1988), p. 212.

the power of the Holy Spirit is a transformed mind. We are, according to Paul, to have "the mind of Christ" (1 Cor 2:16). We are to "have this mind among yourselves, which is yours in Christ Jesus" (Phil 2:5). Similarly, he tells the Romans, "Do not be conformed to this world but be transformed by the renewal of your mind, that you may prove what is the will of God, what is good and acceptable and perfect" (Rom 12:2).

In his letter to the Romans, Paul pins the problem of sin on a darkened intellect (Rom 1:18-23) and places the hope of renewal on a transformed mind (Rom 12:1-2). The problem, according to Paul, arose because of a refusal to worship. The solution springs from a worship that is holy and acceptable to God. Christian meditation in prayer is part of the worship that Paul believed would renew our minds and therefore our hearts.

What is Christian Meditation?

In contrast to meditation techniques aimed at emptying the mind, Christian meditation makes full use of the intellect in an effort to understand God's Word and to hear God's voice. We should not feed our minds a diet that consists largely of the mental junk food of modern media and mindless entertainment. Moreover, our mind, just like our body, needs to be exercised. Thus, St. Paul counsels us to feed our minds with healthy food:

> Finally, brethren, whatever is true, whatever is honorable, whatever is just, whatever is pure, whatever is lovely, whatever is gracious, if there is any excellence, if there is anything worthy of praise, think about these things (Phil 4:8).

That is precisely what Christian meditation is: reflecting on the things that are worth thinking about. It is the work of finding food for the mind, and the most nutritious food of all is the Word of God. This is why the *Catechism of the Catholic Church* tells us: "Meditation is above all a quest. The mind seeks to understand the why and how of the Christian life, in order to adhere and respond to what the Lord is asking" (CCC 2705).

Christian meditation is the pursuit of understanding, starting with the fruits of *lectio.* In our last chapter, we emphasized the importance of careful reading, paying attention to the countless details and patterns found during our *lectio.* But if nothing more is pursued, all we are left with is an inventory of information. Meditation is the time to dig below the surface meaning of the text and ask ourselves "Why does this passage include these particular people? Why are these details noted? Why did the author use this repetition or pattern in their writing?" If *lectio* directs our attention to the "who, what, when, and where" of the passage, meditation seeks understanding by asking "why?" The greater our quest in asking and answering this question in meditation, the more clearly we will hear and encounter God in the later steps of *oratio* and *contemplatio.*

Moving from Lectio to Meditatio with Psalm 1

In our last chapter we "picked the grapes" of Psalm 1, and quickly became aware of how careful *lectio* can reveal a myriad of patterns, repetitions and key words/themes that would not be noted with only a cursory reading of the text.

Such *lectio* prepares the soil for good *meditatio.* So, for instance, while *lectio* notices the three-fold repetition or pattern of "who *walks not in the counsel of the wicked,* nor *stands in the way of sinners,* nor *sits in the seat of scoffers,"* meditation reflects on what this pattern is communicating and teaching. We might reflect that the turning away from holiness and God's ways often happens gradually, with increasing wickedness, until we no longer have the strength to stand and walk away. The move from action to passivity, from walking to sitting, might cause us to reflect on how sin enslaves us. We might also reflect that this truth is a warning for us to be aware of—and on guard against—even the smallest sins so that we can turn away from them with the help of God's grace.

Rather than follow the counsels of the wicked, the blessed man meditates day and night on God's Word. The Hebrew word for meditate, *hagah*, means to reflect upon and, quite often, to vocalize one's ruminations. It connotes an intense, deep reflection. One place where this is vividly portrayed is in the book of Isaiah. The prophet uses the word *hagah*, but in an unexpected way. He uses it to describe the sound the lion makes when eating her prey (Is 31:4). While most English versions translate it as "growls," it is the same Hebrew word used for "meditate" in Psalm 1. Now, most of us don't have lions in our backyard, but we are familiar with this phenomenon. It is the pleasurable purr of your cat as you stroke her back or the sounds of joy your dog makes as he works over a bone. More directly, it is the sound you make as you take that first bite of cheesecake or perfectly cooked steak of the end of your fork. It is an invitation to "delight" in His Word. Like Isaiah's lion, the mind seeks solid meat to meditate on. And once the mind develops the habit of chewing on solid food it won't be satisfied with light fare.

Good *lectio* helps us focus on the key images displayed in a particular text, so much so that we not only "hear" the text, but "see" it with the imagination. At the heart of Psalm 1 stands the arboreal profile, looming tall above all else. Beside this image is the flowing stream, which brings life-giving water. The tree, with its leaves and fruit, relies upon the channels of water. In the arid and hot Middle East, the tree's dependence on the stream for water would be unquestioned.

As I reflect on this scene what comes to mind is my old home in the beautiful Virginia countryside, not far from Shenandoah National Park. We had a huge and ancient oak tree that towered over our house and dominated the four smaller dogwood trees that stood within its shadow. One summer we suffered a drought that was unusual for Virginia's climate, in both duration and severity. The dogwood tree closest to our large oak died, and branches from the others began to die as well. We saved the other dogwoods, whose leaves began to wilt due to the heat and lack of water, because we diligently watered them (although we did this with a watchful eye to make sure that our well did not go dry). What struck me was that the leaves of the oak never wilted or showed the worse for the drought. The oak's deep roots were deep enough to reach the water it needed. That summer and afterward I always thought of that oak as my Psalm 1 tree.

In light of Psalm 1, the grand oak tree became, for me, a parable of the spiritual life. To be rooted in God's Word was to be near the life-giving streams. How many times, I wondered, had I been like the dogwood trees, having a shallow prayer life that exposed me to a lack of nourishment from God's Word. Having experienced more spiritual droughts than I care to admit, I resolve each time I read this psalm to remain rooted in a life of prayer, so as to stay connected to the life-giving water of Sacred Scripture.

In the previous chapter on *lectio* I noted briefly that the image of the righteous man as a tree in Psalm 1 is found throughout Scripture. Psalms 52 and 92 also describe the righteous as a tree, planted in God's temple. This is a rather odd place to be planted, but the image is taken from 1 Kings 6 where the inner sanctuary of Solomon's temple was said to be adorned with the carvings of trees. Why the arboreal imagery in the temple? Because the temple was the new Garden of Eden. Just as the two Cherubim angels guard Eden and its tree of life, so too Solomon's artisans carved two large angels in the inner sanctuary shadowing the Ark of the Covenant.

Reflecting on the details and connections made in *lectio* is what meditation is all about. If the righteous are compared to trees in the psalms, what does it mean for them to be in the Temple? It means that those who pursue the way of the Lord, meditating on His Word, find themselves always to be in the presence of God. The Temple, like Eden, is the place where God's presence is found, and those who meditate on God's law have likewise found the ladder that brings them into God's presence wherever they are in the world. To be rooted in Scripture is to be planted by streams of living water.

When I meditate on Psalm 1 and its arboreal image, I am always intrigued by its possible connection to a tree and rivers in the Garden of Eden. Could it be accidental that the entire Psalter starts out with a prominent tree planted by a river? The allusion to Genesis, which opens with a garden in the midst of which stood the tree of life, planted near a river, seems to beg for further consideration. Could the opening of the Psalter be making an intentional parallel to the opening of the *Torah* (known in Greek as the *Pentateuch* because it consists of the first five books of the Bible)? The rabbis observed that it was fitting that Moses' five books of the Torah had a parallel in

David's five books of psalms, which were the prayerful reflection of praise on God's *torah* ("teaching" or "word").

To be without prayer is to be left parched in the wilderness of the world. However, to be firm in faith against all fear is to be like the tree that stands rooted and unmoved. At least that was the prophet Jeremiah's reflection on Psalm 1, where he says:

> Cursed is the man who trusts in man and makes flesh his arm, whose heart turns away from the LORD. He is like a shrub in the desert, and shall not see any good come. He shall dwell in the parched places of the wilderness, in an uninhabited salt land. Blessed is the man who trusts in the LORD, whose trust is the LORD. He is like a tree planted by water, that sends out its roots by the stream, and does not fear when heat comes, for its leaves remain green, and is not anxious in the year of drought, for it does not cease to bear fruit (Jer 17:5-8).

Jeremiah's meditation on Psalm 1 here takes up a particular angle, that of faith. To trust in the Lord is to be rooted, and when tribulation comes the one who puts his faith in God, and not men, remains unshaken.

We might also ponder the psalmist's image of the blessed man as a tree planted by the waters compared with the chaff of the sinful man. Our meditation might reflect on the fact that chaff is light and easily blown away and that ancient farmers separated wheat from chaff by tossing it in the air allowing the heavy wheat grains to fall to the floor while the lighter chaff was carried away on the wind. And we might contrast this to the blessed man who has *gravitas;* like a tree, he is "heavy," rooted and well-watered. Reflecting on all the noted images and patterns of *lectio* is *meditatio's* work of "squeezing the grapes" of this psalm.

The rich juices of these and other connections can be savored in many different combinations. This process of meditation as "squeezing the juice," informed by the Tradition of the Church and our own study can give us a much richer way of looking at Scripture. In reading Scripture this way there are two things we must keep in mind:

1) We cannot read Scripture in such a way as to violate the Church's faith and morals. (So, for instance, an allegorical reading of Scripture is invalid if it is construed as a justification to commit murder, theft, adultery, etc. or if it is taken to deny some teaching of the Church such as the divinity of Christ or the Real Presence in the Eucharist.)

2) In cases where Scripture or the Church does not attest a particular reading, we cannot demand that fellow Christians agree with our personal interpretation of Scripture.

St. Augustine gives another helpful rule, any interpretation that leads to charity is good, and any reading that works against charity is not. Augustine's rule was an application of Jesus' words about judging whether or not a tree is good, that is, by its fruits (Lk 6:43-44).

With that, I will leave you to practice *meditatio* with Psalm 1 and go on squeezing the grapes a bit more on your own.

A Meditation on Mary and Martha

To give you another sample of meditation, let's explore the following passage from Luke's gospel:

> Now as they went on their way, he entered a village; and a woman named Martha received him into her house. And she had a sister called Mary, who sat at the Lord's feet and listened to his teaching. But Martha was distracted with much serving; and she went to him and said, "Lord, do you not care that my sister has left me

to serve alone? Tell her then to help me." But the Lord answered her, "Martha, Martha, you are anxious and troubled about many things; one thing is needful. Mary has chosen the good portion, which shall not be taken away from her" (Lk 10:38-42).

Using some of the tools we talked about in the previous chapter, let's look for patterns and connections not only within this passage, but within the rest of Scripture, and, as we do so, let's squeeze the juice out in meditation.

It is important to give special attention to the primary words and images in the passage. For instance, we are told Martha "received" Jesus. She is obviously not hostile to Jesus; He is a welcome guest in her family's home. But at the same time, the story clearly wants us to see a difference between Martha and her sister Mary. The difference between the two is not one of opposites, but of degrees. Martha received Jesus, but Mary does more than merely receive, she sat at His feet and listened. She took up a position which any ancient Jew would recognize as profoundly significant: to sit at the feet of one's rabbi is the position of a *disciple*. Paul uses exactly this language to describe his own rabbinic education when he tells his fellow Jews, "I am a Jew, born at Tarsus in Cilicia, but brought up in this city at the feet of Gamaliel" (Acts 22:3). The clear implication is that Mary—a woman—is a model of discipleship.

Mary's posture before the Lord is an example of obedience to God the Father. Jesus teaches about obedient discipleship in the following parable recorded by Luke.

A sower went out to sow his seed; and as he sowed, some fell along the path, and was trodden under foot, and the birds of the air devoured it. And some fell on the rock; and as it grew up, it withered away, because it had no moisture. And some fell among thorns; and the thorns grew with it and choked it. And some fell into good soil and grew, and yielded a hundredfold." As he said this, he called out, "He who has ears to hear, let him hear." And when his disciples asked him what this parable meant, he said, "To you it has been given to know the secrets of the kingdom of God; but for others they are in parables, so that seeing they may not see, and hearing they may not understand. Now the parable is this: The seed is the word of God. The ones along the path are those who have heard; then the devil comes and takes away the word from their hearts, that they may not believe and be saved. And the ones on the rock are those who, when they hear the word, receive it with joy; but these have no root, they believe for a while and in time of temptation fall away. And as for what fell among the thorns, they are those who hear, but as they go on their way they are choked by the cares and riches and pleasures of life, and their fruit does not mature. And as for that in the good soil, they are those who, hearing the word, hold it fast in an honest and good heart, and bring forth fruit with patience" (Lk 8:5-15).

Note the progression Jesus calls for from His disciples. It is not enough to hear the word. It is not even enough to merely receive it with joy. The seed that falls on the path soon withers if it has no root.

As the *Catechism* observes, we need to take up the position of Mary, attentively listening to God's Word:

Christians owe it to themselves to develop the desire to meditate regularly, lest they come to resemble the three first kinds of soil in the parable of the sower. But a method is only a guide; the important thing is to advance, with the Holy Spirit, along the one way of prayer: Christ Jesus (see CCC 2707).

Likewise, Martha's life is "choked by the cares of life." She is doing exactly what a respectable woman is supposed to do in her culture. But Jesus wants her to be more than merely a respectable woman: He wants her to be rich soil for the Word. How does she become this?

God Himself tells us in the chapter before the story of Mary and Martha:

> Now about eight days after these sayings he took with him Peter and John and James, and went up on the mountain to pray. And as he was praying, the appearance of his countenance was altered, and his raiment became dazzling white. And behold, two men talked with him, Moses and Elijah, who appeared in glory and spoke of his departure, which he was to accomplish at Jerusalem. Now Peter and those who were with him were heavy with sleep, and when they wakened they saw his glory and the two men who stood with him. And as the men were parting from him, Peter said to Jesus, "Master, it is well that we are here; let us make three booths, one for you and one for Moses and one for Elijah," not knowing what he said. As he said this, a cloud came and overshadowed them; and they were afraid as they entered the cloud. And a voice came out of the cloud, saying, "This is my Son, my Chosen; listen to him!" (Lk 9:28-35)

To be a true disciple, it is not enough to simply receive Jesus as Martha does, you must *listen* to Him. This is why the *Shema*, the great commandment of Deuteronomy 6:4-5, automatically links hearing God with doing His will. It is also why Jesus says repeatedly, "He who has ears to hear, let him hear." If we are listening to Him, we are ready and willing to obey. Mary fulfils God's command by listening attentively to the Lord.

Martha, in contrast, was "anxious and troubled about many things." She was so busy doing for Jesus and her guests that she was doing everything but the "one thing needful." And again, we find a connection between what Jesus tells her and what He tells us all:

> And he said to his disciples, "Therefore I tell you, do not be anxious about your life, what you shall eat, nor about your body, what you shall put on. For life is more than food, and the body more than clothing. Consider the ravens: they neither sow nor reap, they have neither storehouse nor barn, and yet God feeds them. Of how much more value are you than the birds! And which of you by being anxious can add a cubit to his span of life? . . . And do not seek what you are to eat and what you are to drink, nor be of anxious mind. For all the nations of the world seek these things; and your Father knows that you need them. Instead, seek his kingdom, and these things shall be yours as well" (Lk 12:22-25, 29-31).

An astute reader of Luke will hear the repetition of the word "anxious" and note that it is being flagged for emphasis. This should then recall earlier uses of this word, particularly Jesus' rebuke of Martha's anxiety. By connecting repetition of "anxious," we observe that Jesus wants us to uproot this noxious weed that chokes out faith and love. We then can turn and reflect upon what makes us anxious, and keeps us from the one thing needful.

Although Jesus takes exception to Martha, His rebuke is gentle. Notice that He repeats Martha's name, which is characteristic for Jesus when He is speaking to those He loves. He will, indeed, do the same for Peter on the night Peter abandons Him (Lk 22:31) and when He calls the rebellious Saul to repentance (Acts 9:4). He defends and protects Mary—and calls Martha to join them in the "one thing needful." The language Jesus uses is, once again, deeply significant, because He says that Mary has chosen the "good portion." Even that simple term has real significance. Under the Levitical system, the priests were not given large tracts of land like the other tribes. Instead, they received a special "portion" of the sacrifices to live on. As time went on, meditation on the Law of Moses revealed to Israel that God was the *real* portion being shared in the sacrifices. So, for instance, Psalm 16 sings:

> The Lord is my chosen portion and my cup;
> Thou holdest my lot.
> The lines have fallen for me in pleasant places;
> Yea, I have a goodly heritage.

This psalm speaks, not of the grain offering or the goat's meat as the portion, not of any plot of land measured out, but of God Himself as the true inheritance of Israel. Peter tells us that it is a psalm of praise by which the Messiah thanks God for His Resurrection (Acts 2:25-31).

It is a theme repeated many times throughout the book of Psalms.

> Whom have I in heaven but thee?
> And there is nothing upon earth that I desire besides thee.
> My flesh and my heart may fail,
> but God is the strength of my heart and my portion for
> ever (Ps 73:25-26).

> The LORD is my portion;
> I promise to keep thy words (Ps 119:57).
>
> I cry to thee, O LORD; I say,
> Thou art my refuge,
> my portion in the land of the living (Ps 142:5).

Jesus' use of this specific phrase clearly indicates that Mary has chosen God Himself, and this shall not be taken away from her. Implied in His rebuke, however, is not that Martha is banished, but that she, too, is invited to drop her harried anxiety and sit at His feet so that she might also receive the "good portion," God Himself.

The *Catechism* quotes St. Thérèse of Lisieux's reflection on this passage about Mary and Martha. It gives us a glimpse of how the saints, with careful reading of Scripture, cultivate a fruitful meditation that moves from the mind to the heart: "But above all it's the Gospels that occupy my mind when I'm at prayer; my poor soul has so many needs, and yet this is the one thing needful. I'm always finding fresh lights there, hidden and enthralling meanings" (CCC 127). Thérèse's allusion to Martha's "many needs" in contrast to Mary's "one thing needful" is obvious. By deeply meditating on this story Thérèse planted herself by the streams of living water, and she bore amazing fruit indeed.

God is Speaking to You!

At this point we need to remember the "secret" of the saints from our earlier chapter. It is very easy, and indeed fitting, to read about Mary and Martha and the tension between them with a sort of fond affection. They are like two beloved aunts. The story of Jesus and His intervention in this little family dispute draws a wry smile from us. But if we just leave the story there, as an old family anecdote, we miss the most crucial point: that these things were written for *our* benefit under the inspiration of the Holy Spirit. In short, this story is God's Word *to each of us*. He is speaking through it to you and me.

That is why St. Thérèse habitually put her name in place of Martha's. *You* are the one who is worried and distracted about many things. *You* are the one who is called to sit at Jesus' feet. Having meditated with the mind on some of the many connections this story has with the rest of the Word of God, it is necessary to go deeper lest we "receive the word with joy" but have the seed gobbled up by birds along the path. We need to avail ourselves of it lest, like Martha, we allow the seed to be "choked by the cares and riches and pleasures of life," which would prevent *our* fruit from maturing. The point of our meditation is not simply to note some facts about a couple of quarrelling sisters who spoke a strange language and died long ago. The point of our meditation is that, here and now, we become the good soil, like those "who, hearing the word, hold it fast in an honest and good heart, and bring forth fruit with patience."

There are numerous insights to meditate on in any passage of Scripture. The goal of meditation is not to reflect on the highest number of items, but rather to go where the Spirit leads us. During our *lectio* or *meditatio*, our heart might be stirred by one particular observation. Stop there. Don't just continue onto the next thing. Take time to go deeper and let the Holy Spirit move your *meditatio* to the next stage of your journey through *lectio divina*. It is what some call the longest road in the world. But with God's help we can take it, full of confidence that many saints before us have trodden it successfully.

It is the journey from the head to the heart, and we shall go via the royal highway known as *oratio*.

Chapter Five

Oratio

The diligent reading of Sacred Scripture accompanied by prayer brings about the intimate dialogue in which the person reading hears God who is speaking, and in praying, responds to him with trusting openness of heart.

— Pope Benedict XVI

The approach to Scripture via *lectio divina* immediately addresses one of the things many people find most frustrating about prayer: having a clue what to pray about. When we are trying to begin a conversation with God we can forget what we always instinctively understand with each other: that a conversation must be *about* something. We don't sit down, look at each other, and say "Let's have a really good talk." If we did, the result would likely be several minutes of long and uncomfortable silence. Instead, we talk about a particular question, issue, or subject that means a lot to us.

In *lectio* and *meditatio*, we have collected and squeezed the grapes and begun to discover that a great many weighty matters are dealt with even in a seemingly small portion of Scripture. And as we do so, we almost can't help noticing that many of those matters bear directly on our own life. It is here that *oratio* begins.

So, for instance, as we read the story of Mary and Martha, we may begin to notice certain uncomfortable similarities between

Martha and ourselves, or certain happy similarities between Mary and ourselves. A while back, as I was reflecting on the story of Mary and Martha, another passage came to mind, one that has often haunted me, a passage from Sirach 11:10: "My son, do not busy yourself with many matters; if you multiply activities you will not go unpunished, and if you pursue you will not overtake, and by fleeing you will not escape." It is not hard to recognize that this is true, not simply for a first-century woman in a small village who received Jesus into her home, but of our own lives right here and now.

So we should take that word to prayer and ask God to help us see how we may have driven ourselves to the "punishment" of distraction. We ask the Spirit to help us examine our conscience and go over our actions to see where in our lives we are like Martha, worried about many things and neglectful of the "one thing." We talk to God about the things we pursue and don't overtake, the unfinished tasks, the unfulfilled hopes and dreams that lie about us because we did not focus on the one thing needful, instead running hither and yon in distraction. We speak to God about the things we are fleeing in fear, the things that drive us away from the one thing to which He calls us.

Perhaps we don't know what the "one thing" is. We don't know what God would have us do or be. We talk to Him about that and ask Him to reveal to us whatever the next practical step is. We hold up Scripture as a light to examine our life and expect that, because it is God's Word to us, He will speak to us.

As we grow in knowledge of Scripture and deepen our meditation, we may start to ask deeper questions. Do we sit at Jesus' feet during the celebration of the Mass, or are our minds distracted fretting about what so-and-so is wearing and demanding that Jesus tell them to dress more appropriately like ourselves? Do we focus on the one thing like Mary or do we find that our life is full of things we never finish (or even start) because we are distracted? Do we find when we try to relax that all the things we have left undone bother us? Even our distractions can be helpful, as they show us what we are attached to and can signal subjects that we should submit to God.[22] In *oratio* we bring all this to God in prayer. And if we find that the passage we are meditating on doesn't seem to have anything to do with our life (but does remind us of someone else we are concerned about), we bring that to God too.

The point of all this is neither to kick yourself if you recognize some sin or failing, nor to boast if you discover some growing virtue. Rather, it is to bring what you find in Scripture into contact with your own life and speak truthfully to God about what you see there. It is also to listen to the word with open ears, mind and heart. The key is to remain in relationship with God as you mull over the connections and implications your meditation on Scripture has for your life and for the lives of those around you.

---

[22] The *Catechism* offers some wonderful advice on this issue of distraction: "To set about hunting down distractions would be to fall into their trap, when all that is necessary is to turn back to our heart: for a distraction reveals to us what we are attached to, and this humble awareness before the Lord should awaken our preferential love for him and lead us resolutely to offer him our heart to be purified" (CCC 2729).

The Biblical Pattern

In all this, we see what we are to be about as we step onto the *oratio* rung of the *lectio divina* ladder and talk with Jesus about the things He has shown us through *lectio* and *meditatio*. It is the moment when we start to talk through our questions, puzzlement, wonder, fear, complaints, and happiness regarding the things we discover on the sacred page. In so doing, we imitate Christ's greatest disciple, the Blessed Virgin Mary, who "kept all these things in her heart" (Luke 2:51) where they fermented like fine wine. In *oratio* we talk with God about the word He has spoken in Scripture and seek how it may be applied to our lives as a word spoken *to us*.

If we don't know where to start, Scripture itself provides us with many examples. One of the first things to remember, for instance, is that Paul tells us that the Old Testament Scriptures were "written down for our instruction, upon whom the end of the ages has come" (1 Cor 10:11). That means we can look at the Old Testament models who show us how to pray, and imitate them. And one of the first things we see when we do this is how unafraid they are to ask God questions. Abraham, for instance, often confronts God with questions. In fact, at one point he famously enters into a hard-nosed negotiation with God in classic Middle Eastern fashion to see how few righteous men need to be in Sodom in order to save the city from destruction (Gn 18:17-33).

Wrestling with God

In the same way, other venerable figures of the Old Testament offer prayers of praise and petition, but they also chew things over with God. Another great model for this is Jacob, who has a memorable encounter on his way back to the Holy Land, where he hopes to be reconciled with Esau:

> And Jacob was left alone; and a man wrestled with him until the breaking of the day. When the man saw that he did not prevail against Jacob, he touched the hollow of his thigh; and Jacob's thigh was put out of joint as he wrestled with him. Then he said, "Let me go, for the day is breaking." But Jacob said, "I will not let you go, unless you bless me." And he said to him, "What is your name?" And he said, "Jacob." Then he said, "Your name shall no more be called Jacob, but Israel, for you have striven with God and with men, and have prevailed." Then Jacob asked him, "Tell me, I pray, your name." But he said, "Why is it that you ask my name?" And there he blessed him. So Jacob called the name of the place Peniel, saying, "For I have seen God face to face, and yet my life is preserved." The sun rose upon him as he passed Peniel, limping because of his thigh. Therefore to this day the Israelites do not eat the sinew of the hip which is upon the hollow of the thigh, because he touched the hollow of Jacob's thigh on the sinew of the hip (Gn 32:24-32).

This characterizes the biblical approach to prayer in a profound way. In the struggle Jacob's name is changed to Israel, which means "he who struggles with God." Of course Jacob's twelve sons become twelve tribes who take their national name from their great forefather, Israel. The collective name of God's people, Israel, is itself an invitation to wrestle with God.

The boldness of this name can be contrasted to the origin of the term Islam, which means "submission," and to Islamic prayer, in which you simply bow before God and accept whatever is spoken or done as the act of Allah. To question is to transgress. Your only allowable response is to pray and say "God is great!" and probe no further into the mystery of God's inscrutable will.

In stark contrast, the patriarchs, biblical prophets, apostles, and even Jesus Himself *wrestled* with God in prayer. That is why we see them so frequently asking what God is doing, or why they are facing some trial, wondering about the meaning of some sign, or crying out "Father, if it is possible, let this cup pass from me ..." God's Word compels us to explore the gamut of human experience, not to ignore it. We are to remain in relationship with God, not read Scripture or live life as though God were not intimately involved. It all hinges on how you see God. If He is a Master defined as being over and against His creation, you relate as a slave to a suzerain. But, if you see God as a loving Father, you know you can approach Him with filial boldness and the reckless abandon of a young boy jumping into the arms of his father, knowing that His strength will always protect you.

Jacob gives God's people a model, a kind of permission to wrestle with the Lord. But that does not mean that we will always win, and even when Jacob did, he left with a limp. Jeremiah laments of this when he decries how God has duped him (the root of Jacob's name means "to deceive," a point the prophet is alluding to) into doing what Jeremiah was reluctant to do from the start, that is, playing the role of a prophet to Jerusalem. Unlike Jacob, Jeremiah does not feel all that blessed by the encounter with God and, in words clearly aimed to contrast his lot with Jacob's says," O Lord, you have deceived me, and I was deceived; you are stronger than I, and you have prevailed" (Jeremiah 20:7). As Jeremiah understood from personal experience, you can wrestle with God but you don't always win. The great thing about reading the book of Jeremiah is to see that even while the prophet is often pinned, he doesn't give up in his struggle to understand and love the Lord in spite of all the tears and terror he endures.

The Psalms: Mirror of the Soul

St. Athanasius once observed that the Psalms are like a mirror of the soul. This means that in the Psalms you can find all the emotions and passions of human life. In Psalm 89, for instance, we read one of the great "psalms of complaint" in which the psalmist asks every question we have ever asked when God has allowed something painful and baffling to crash into our life. It begins as a psalm of praise to God and recounts the many blessings and promises He gave to the House of David. But then the psalmist goes on to ask, "What happened?" Everything has come crashing down, David's kingdom has fallen, the people of God are on the ropes, and God seems to be nowhere in sight: "Lord, where is thy steadfast love of old, which by thy faithfulness thou didst swear to David?" (Ps 89:49).

It is a question that is asked, neither in anger or despair, nor in derision or ridicule. It is asked, rather, in faith; in the determination to stay with God until an answer comes, whether in this life or the next. That's why the psalm ends with "Blessed be the LORD for ever! Amen and Amen" (Ps 89:52). The psalmist *wrestled* with God. He does not simply bow in mute submission as Islam commands, nor does he simply stomp off in contempt for God as modern atheism demands. He *stays* with God and expects an answer.

The Gospels: Conversation with Christ

The apostles do much the same thing when Jesus says the various shocking, beautiful, and sometimes unexpected things that constitute His teaching. The apostles ask Him all sorts of questions and aren't afraid to even ask dumb questions, or questions that shock modern piety. Peter, in particular, has no hesitation about saying whatever he thinks or is struggling to understand. He tells Jesus he believes He is the Christ—and is commended by Jesus for it (see Mt 16:15-17). He tells Jesus He shouldn't suffer and die—and is rebuked by Jesus for it (see Mt 16:22-23). He doesn't understand Jesus' words about the Bread of Life, but he also says "Lord, to whom shall we go? You have the words of eternal life!" (Jn 6:68). He is, for us modern church-going folk, embarrassingly forward when he asks Jesus "What's in it for us?" (see Mt 19:27). Yet Jesus does not rebuke him for doing so. The whole point here is that the apostles knew they could talk to Jesus about anything

As we read through the gospels we should realize that every conversation with Jesus is a lesson in prayer, for prayer is a dialogue with God. Once we comprehend this invaluable lesson, we can read these stories profitably. So, when Jesus encounters the father whose son is possessed by demons which the disciples were unable to cast out, the man then turns to Jesus and says, "If you can do anything, have pity on us and help us." (Mk 9:22). Jesus picks up the man's slim confidence, understandable in light of the apostles' failure, and exclaims, "*If you can!* All things are possible to him who believes" (Mk 9:23, emphasis added). Immediately the father cries out to Christ, "I believe; help my unbelief!" (Mk 9:24). This simple reply is striking for its stark honesty. And here is the lesson: what matters most in speaking with Christ is not pious words and platitudes, but the honest expression from the depth of our heart.

Throughout all the conversations with Christ in the gospels, we can commit to memory many lines well worth remembering; phrases that we can recycle into our own conversations with God. Whether it is the words of the publican, "God, be merciful to me a sinner!" (Lk 18:13); or the cry of the blind man Bartimaeus, "Jesus, Son of David, have mercy on me!" (Mk 10:47); or the request of the Samaritan woman, "Give me this water, that I may not thirst" (Jn 4:15); or the plea of the leper, "Lord, if you will, you can make me clean" (Mt 8:2); or the reply of Martha "Yes, Lord; I believe that you are the Christ" (Jn 11:27); or the noble statement of the centurion, "Lord, I am not worthy to have you come under my roof; but only say the word, and my servant will be healed" (Mt 8:8); or the Peter's pithy prayer "Lord, save me!" (Mt 14:30), all of these lines express the heart's deepest needs and feelings to God.

The monks who practiced *lectio divina* carefully recorded in their personal notebooks or journals the key verses that struck them in prayer or liturgy. Like a honeybee collecting nectar, they would gather these precious Scripture passages for further meditation. As the monks did this they came up with a further practical insight, they realized it helped to write down, slowly, these precious Scripture passages that spoke to them, so that they could be etched into their hearts.

In this way, the monks would memorize a passage and return to it while they worked with their hands and as they were doing the duties of the day. This is a wonderful exercise! I suggest that you take a verse that really draws you in and write it down slowly and carefully on a 3"x 5" note card or in a simple journal. Carry it around with you and read and reread it until you memorize it. I use a small notebook that fits into my pocket. I take it with me everywhere, and I write down verses and insights gathered in prayer so that like the monks I can return to it and "taste and see the goodness of the Lord," for His Word is "sweeter also than honey and the drippings of the honeycomb" (Ps 19:10).

As you read through the gospel accounts of people's conversations with Christ, you will notice that what marks Jesus' approach is this: *He does not answer the question, He answers the questioner.* Or to put it a little differently, He is never content to leave us at the level of the superficial or the merely intellectual. He aims to give us truth, not merely facts. He demands the response of the whole person, particularly the heart. In every conversation, He is calling us into a deeper relationship with Himself. And He confronts us with the same call to relationship. This is why *lectio divina* must pass from *meditatio* to *oratio*: we have to let the Holy Spirit apply the Word to our lives.

Overcoming Obstacles

Many people can start to lose nerve at this point. For some (particularly laypeople), the fear is simply stated as "That's for saints. I can't do that."

By "can't," if you mean that "the Church disapproves of the laity doing this. I'm trespassing on the territory of the experts," we have it on the highest Church authority that you are mistaken. Pope Benedict XVI, as quoted at the beginning of this chapter, and Pope John Paul II are of one mind here. As Pope John Paul II told us in his 1996 *Post-Synodal Exhortation on the Consecrated Life*, in *lectio divina*:

> The word of God is brought to bear on life, on which it projects that light of wisdom which is a gift of the Spirit

… Indeed it would be helpful if this practice were also encouraged among other members of the People of God, priests *and laity alike* (no. 94, emphasis added).

The Holy Father's point here is simple: God's Word is spoken to *all* of His people.

Another common fear is the notion that not being a "master" of *lectio divina* means you can never start. It's what we are really saying when we say things like, "I could never make all those connections and cross-references you were making when you were talking about Psalm 1 and or Mary and Martha." Again, the answer is straightforward: You also can't run a marathon the first day you put on your sneakers. But nobody is asking you to. St. Gregory the Great once said that Scripture is a river whose depths depends on the one who walks within it: a lamb can wade in and an elephant can drown. Most of us are like the lamb, yet that is no reason to not get your feet wet.

The bottom line is if you can read, you can read Scripture—and that's enough to get started. It takes practice to get to know Scripture and make the connections. But as you do, you discover a growing confidence and certain habits and skills become second nature, just as they do when you learn to drive. Eventually, you reach the point where your conversation with God moves to a deeper level because you are no longer focused on things like "Where is the book of Proverbs again?" Instead, you find you are looking at how this passage from Proverbs throws new light on that thought of Paul's—and how God is speaking to you through it all.

So don't worry about being a beginner. Happily, God is easy to please but hard to satisfy. That means He will accept even our faltering steps if we are only willing to try. It also means that He will never stop calling us "further up and further in" to His revelation and we must persevere.

In the Heart of the Church

The radical expectation behind *lectio divina* is that God *will speak to you*. The Fathers of the Church are blunt: "When you pray, you speak with God; when you read, God speaks to you."[23] That's heady stuff and no small reason why many Catholics feel nervous about trying it. What frightens us is that we are going to botch it and misunderstand what God is speaking to us. But what we need to remember is this: God will speak, but He will not speak or command anything that contradicts the faith and morals of the Church. Scripture is a word that has been entrusted to the Church. It is the Church, according to Scripture that is the "pillar and bulwark of the truth" (1 Tm 3:15). For that reason, it is entirely appropriate and necessary to make sure that our *lectio divina* is done in the context of the whole revelation of Christ.

The habit of the true Catholic heart and mind is not to avoid praying Scripture but instead to always check one's discernment of God's Word with the teaching of the Church. Public revelation ended with the death of the last apostle, St. John. However, just because public revelation is concluded with the New Testament, it does not mean that God does not want to communicate to each and every one of us at the deep and intimate level of the heart. Indeed, the *Catechism* observes that "The Holy Spirit, whose anointing permeates our whole being, is the interior Master of Christian prayer. He is the artisan of the living tradition of prayer... [and] it is the same Spirit acting in all

---

[23] St. Cyprian, *Ad Donatum*, 15: CCL IIIA, 12

and with all" (CCC 2672). The same Holy Spirit who inspired God's Word in Scripture wants to inspire your prayer.

True, the devil exists and he loves to trick us by appealing to our fears, desires, and weaknesses. And the temptation in the desert makes clear, the devil does not hesitate to cite Scripture if it suits his purposes (Lk 4:9-12). But none of that is a reason to avoid *lectio divina*. Rather, as Jesus himself demonstrates by His own citations of Scripture in answer to the devil, it's the reason to do *lectio divina* as the Church teaches we should do it: in the bosom of Holy Mother Church. If we keep our meditation, prayer and discernment of God's Word centered in the full teaching of the Church, we will be fine.

One final point: many people get stuck at *oratio* because they simply don't know how to pray and they are ashamed of it. Often what lies at the heart of this hesitation is the notion that we are oddballs and everybody else *does* know how to pray. But the reality is quite otherwise. Remember the first thing St. Paul tells *all* of us about prayer is that *none* of us knows how to do it: "For we do not know how to pray as we ought, but the Spirit himself intercedes for us with sighs too deep for words" (Rom 8:26).

And that, in turn, leads us to what may be for us, in our culture which relies so much on the know-how of experts, the uncomfortable truth that prayer must include both the Holy Spirit and us. Like the wind, the Spirit blows where He wills. We cannot bottle, contain, control or tame God's Spirit. When it fell on King Saul he did some crazy things, and when it fell at Pentecost, outsiders thought that the Christians were drunk. Being open to the Spirit means going on an adventure, and we don't always get to chart the course.

One Last Step

As you open yourself to the Holy Spirit, you will be led deeper into the love of God, not merely as the source of good things, but as Goodness Himself. That will be the moment you put your foot on the next rung of the Divine Ladder: *contemplatio.*

Chapter Six

Contemplatio

Contemplation comes from a deeply personal contact with God, and that is why method is the least useful at the point where prayer is the most personal.
— Jacques Philippe

Contemplation is when the mind is in some sort lifted up to God and held above itself, so that it tastes the joys of everlasting sweetness.
... Reading seeks for the sweetness of a blessed life, meditation perceives it, prayer asks for it, contemplation tastes it.
— Guigo the Carthusian

The progression from *lectio* to *meditatio* to *oratio* to *contemplatio* is one from sense, to intellect, to affect, and then to the capturing of all those powers by God in something that transcends them. The first three steps require arduous effort, the last is effortless and yet beyond all our abilities of mind and will. Like gardening, prayer takes planting, tending, and harvest before we taste the fruits of our labors. Like a long hike up a mountain, where each step is challenged by an ever-growing incline, the first few steps up Guigo's ladder require an effort that can only be sustained by a firm purpose and perseverance. Yet, if you keep putting one foot in front of the other, you will reach, somewhere above the tree line, the long-awaited peak. A mountain hike is full of rewards along the way—from wildlife to wildflowers

—but none compare to the joy of reaching the top of the world, where you are granted a vision beyond what you could possibly take in or even remember in any of its dizzying breadth or detail. In that moment of restful peace, where you gaze in wonder at a view that takes your breath away as much as the thin air, you experience, I am convinced, something akin to the vision of contemplation. After all the labor of *lectio*, all the mindfulness of *meditatio*, and all the fervor of *oratio, contemplatio* is a restful gaze upon the Author of all beauty and wonder.

A Gaze of Love

Several years ago, I delivered a lecture on *lectio divina* at a Catholic college. After my talk a discerning student asked me a simple but important question: how would I define contemplation? Perceptively, she had picked up on my Achilles' heal. I tried to dodge the question, claiming that the best definition of contemplation is that it is indefinable, but she pressed the point and I palpably felt the inadequacy of my attempted answers. Indeed, I felt the truth of St. Augustine's observation that it is easy to think you understand something until someone asks you to explain it; it is only then that you discover just how threadbare your thought is. Nonetheless, her curiosity spurred a deeper curiosity in me. Over the months that followed I tried to read on the topic whenever I had a free moment, but I soon found that I was as dissatisfied as the young woman had been. It seemed that many of the authors were lost in abstractions or simply described contemplation as beyond description.

Some months later I came upon the answer, but not in my study or in one of my many books. It came late one night when I wandered into my son's room before heading to bed for some long-awaited shut-eye. I saw my son, with the moonlight illuminating his sleeping figure; his hands were crossed over his chest, with a teddy bear tucked close by, and his face radiated an angelic serenity. It was one of those precious moments when time seems suspended. My eyes were fixed upon this scene of beauty and my heart leaped for love, a love that brought the strongest emotions of joy and peace. As I stood there staring, for I don't know how long, I perceived that I was lost in contemplation. This, I realized, is what contemplation is: *a gaze of love.*

Shortly after my moonlit vision of *contemplatio* our family enjoyed one of our much-beloved hikes in the Rocky Mountains. Each time we hiked that year I thought about contemplation, and how the beauty I could see was a sacrament of that Love which first imagined and then created all that I saw. As we wandered up winding paths past innumerable wild flowers, I felt a new appreciation for the brilliant red of the Scarlet Gilia Fairy Trumpet, with its five-pointed lobes that look like they have exploded in a fireworks show; the majestic purple of the Fireweed, robed in a purple more royal than anything Solomon ever donned; the baby blue of the Early Larkspur and the Wild Blue Flax; the cluster of luminous white flowers that show forth Jacob's Ladder (yes, there is a wildflower with this name, and it is fun reflecting on how this flower is connected to the Patriarch's ladder), and the fire-red Indian Paintbrush (its vibrant color and my childhood love of Indians makes it my personal favorite). My son knows how much I enjoy Indian Paintbrush, so whenever he comes upon it he announces his discovery as though he has found treasure; and treasure indeed it is! To gaze upon the beauty of these floral treasures that are found in such abundance to those who make but a little effort to ascend the mountain heights was another form of contemplation, a deepened experience of the Love that had brought forth the glorious beauty of creation.

Each of us has experienced something akin to the gift of contemplation in our daily lives and relationships, whether it is the silent joy of looking at a child in restful slumber, or the carefree joy of play; or the peaceful joy of holding hands with one we love, of watching a spectacular sunset spread its glorious hues across the horizon, or of hiking amidst the glory of a field of wildflowers; or the silent awe when gazing upon the artist's work that takes a simple canvas and transforms it to a marvel of beauty—indeed, it is the vocation of art to help us become contemplatives, to see the beauty of creation and respond to it as St. Francis of Assisi did, with the contemplative praise and joy that filled his being. In every life, there are moments when words would spoil the moment, when the thing to do is simply to gaze in wonder, to "behold the beauty of the LORD" (Ps 27:4).

What is my point in all this? The heart of what I am saying is made clear by a great German philosopher, Josef Pieper, whose essay on contemplation I discovered with a joy similar to that of coming upon a vibrant wildflower while on an alpine hike.

> Only the vision of something we love makes us happy, and thus it is integral to the concept of contemplation that it represents a vision kindled by the act of turning towards something in love and affirmation ... We need to be expressly reassured of the fact that many of the experiences we have in the course of our day-to-day lives are in fact worthy of all the praise which has always been justly accorded to the contemplative life. We also need corroboration and confirmation of the fact that

we are right to interpret and accept the beatitude of such experiences for what it truly is: the foretaste and beginning of perfect joy.[24]

The ability to experience natural contemplation prepares the way for divine contemplation. My contemplation and joy of the beauty of God's creation and of the gift of my son are preparation for, and the foretaste of, the spiritual contemplation of God Himself. And today many of us need to hear the message of the forerunner before we are ready for the advent of the fuller revelation God wants to give.

Similarly, St. Thomas Aquinas' *meditatio* on Scripture and communion with God prepared him for an experience of *contemplatio* so profound that when St. Thomas surveyed his massive contribution to Christian theology and philosophy after an extraordinary encounter with God in prayer, he remarked, "All that I have written seems to me like straw compared with what has now been revealed to me." His point was not that his work was worthless, but rather that God is infinitely sweeter; not to mention that the experience of God goes beyond even the most brilliant account of the greatest minds.

St. Thomas Aquinas taught that "grace builds on nature." Grace, like water, needs the soil of nature to do its work. True, the visible can veil what is invisible, but the believer who prays learns to see the natural world as a sacrament of the supernatural. If we can get our minds around what natural contemplation consists of, like gazing in wonder at the graceful form of Scarlet Gilia Fairy Trumpet, it gives us a crucial analogy for understanding what theologians call

---

[24] See Josef Pieper's wonderful essay on contemplation, "Earthly Contemplation," in *Josef Pieper: An Anthology* (San Francisco: Ignatius, 1989), pp. 144-145.

infused contemplation; contemplation of a much higher order. Thus, contemplation of this world's beauty prepares us for and helps us understand what it might mean to contemplate the Love that moves the sun, the moon, and the stars.

Taste and See

As you practice *lectio divina* and read and meditate on God's Word, your mind falls in love with the truth. And as you realize that the truth is not a mere collection of facts, but the Gift of a Lover to you, His beloved, you begin to experience rapture. Rather than the fizzy soda pop of New Age faddishness, *contemplatio* gives us the fine mature wine of the Holy Spirit – and we rejoice singing "You have put more joy in my heart than they have when their grain and wine abound. In peace I will both lie down and sleep; for you alone, O LORD, make me dwell in safety" (Ps 4:7-8). The psalmist proclaims, "Take delight in the LORD, and he will give you the desires of your heart" (Psalm 37:4), and in *contemplatio* we receive "the" desire of our heart, God Himself. The point is this: if you truly delight in the Lord, then He will give you *Himself*! And He is joy and love!

The initial steps of *lectio divina* take us into the text of Scripture and on an adventure where we are cast in a demanding role and act upon Scripture's text with our mind, will, and heart. In these early stages we hear and dialogue with God's Word in Scripture; but now, in *contemplatio*, we move beyond interaction with God through His Word to the experience of God Himself. In the last stage the syntax of prayer is reversed, as the believer who was the praying subject becomes the object of God's action. During contemplation we become the receiver, with God, so to speak, acting within and upon us.

This is what spiritual writers call infused contemplation. It usually begins with what is called the prayer of quiet, in which our powers rest and God uses this state of tranquil attentiveness to offer the soul a simple taste of Himself. Put simply: contemplation is a gaze of love. Indeed, the Saints describe contemplation as a love that transcends the passion of love. It is a kind of swoon. It is common for people to speak of the contemplative experience as a refined appreciation for the things that God has created, and that is true, but the Saints often describe it as a wordless experience of God who is the Author of it all.

Describing the Indescribable

Contemplation gives us a refined draught, a drink that inebriates us with unspeakable joy. Our friend Guigo the Carthusian describes contemplation through a series of metaphors as follows:

> Reading, as it were, puts food whole into the mouth, meditation chews it and breaks it up, prayer extracts its flavor, *contemplation is the sweetness itself which gladdens and refreshes.* Reading works on the outside, meditation on the pith: prayer asks for what we long for, *contemplation gives us delight in the sweetness* which we have found … *Contemplation when it comes rewards the labors of the other three; it inebriates the thirsting soul with the dew of heavenly sweetness* (emphasis added).

But many today feel a great deal of embarrassment at the idea that we might experience, much less talk about, "the sweetness and delight of contemplation." The proposition that "contemplation tastes and inebriates" is something that fills many with distinct unease. Such language, however, is not an exhibit of irrational exuberance, but rather the grasping attempt of a lover trying to put his experience of love in words. Here the problem is not with the experience or the speaker, but rather with the poor wineskins of human language that burst in their attempt to contain and describe a potent love.

Repeatedly, the encounter with God takes us to a place beyond words. The psalmist puts it this way, "Look to him, and be radiant" (Ps 34:5). The Song of Solomon exclaims, "My heart was thrilled within me" (Sng 5:4). These are not the words of a philosopher or a logician. They are the words of a lover, a mystic and, mark this, a human being, whose nature is made up of spirit and flesh. Indeed, a later psalm describes our longing for God not with an abstract theological discourse on the concepts of Truth and Beauty, but by singing, "As a hart [deer] longs for flowing streams, so longs my soul for you, O God" (Ps 42:1). The psalmist compares the desire of the saints, not to the abstractions of the philosophers, but to the thirst of a deer.

We may well ask "Why does the psalmist describe the experience of God with such a clearly physical reality?" I suspect the answer is found both in what we are, and in the way in which God has chosen to reveal Himself. Human beings are fallen rational animals. We are created in the image and likeness of God, with both a spiritual soul and a physical body. While our bodies hunger, bleed, and tire, our rational souls are capable of seeing things far beyond our mere feelings, appetites and sense experience.

When God chose to reveal Himself to fallen humanity He did so not as a spirit without a body, or as a brain in a jar, but by taking on human nature, with flesh, blood, hands, feet, feelings, and appetites: He "became flesh and dwelt among us" (Jn 1:14). The Risen Christ both beheld the face of His Father and ate fish. The Resurrection glorified, not annihilated, human nature. When God makes His supreme revelation known to us, He does so, not by starting a school of philosophy, but by becoming a helpless baby. When He climaxes that revelation, it is not by Jesus preaching a great philosophical treatise in a seminar, but by the raw physical spectacle of a man beaten "beyond human semblance" (Is 52:14) and left to die bleeding on a gibbet, followed by the mystery of that very same body raised to a glory that cannot be told adequately by any human language.

When God speaks to us in the Mass, the movement of the Church's public worship is not from the Liturgy of the Word to the Liturgy of Still More Words, but to the Liturgy Beyond Words—the Eucharist. In the most intimate encounter with God possible in this life, God does not say "Take and understand," but "Take and eat." Indeed, this physical experience of tasting God in the Eucharist stands behind the reason the medievals made much of the association between *sapor* and *sapientia*, the Latin terms for "taste or flavor" and "wisdom," respectively. At its highest, wisdom is not so much an articulate cognitive experience but is more akin to the savor of a flavor on the tongue—with all the Eucharistic overtones that this suggests. The image implies that the tongue moves from speaking to simple tasting. This captures well the unusual road of contemplation, which moves from the intellectual labor of reading, meditation, and verbal prayer to the wordless experience of God Himself. Here the Eucharist provides a paradigm for understanding how contemplation transcends the mind in the embrace of love.

Contemplation, in the technical spiritual sense, is a terribly difficult thing to describe, because it has God as its subject and object—and God is not easily defined, or tamed. But in His wisdom, God chose the bodily act of eating (in the Eucharist) as a vehicle to communion with

Him. And so, poignantly, both the psalmist in the Old Testament and the Christian tradition make use of the natural aspects of our being when attempting to put into words the very "super-natural" aspects of our encounter with God.

The Ladder to Contemplation

In the first three stages of *lectio divina* the mind is very active, working diligently to draw from the wellspring of Scripture the themes and ideas that nourish meditation and then conversing with God about these things. The fourth stage, however, comes to us like a gentle rain or the slow descent of falling snowflakes. In contemplation, we need not water the spiritual garden of our prayer by our own efforts of irrigation, for God Himself provides all we need. In terms of effort, contemplation is as different from the first three stages as an elevator is to a ladder. In the labor of *lectio-meditatio-oratio* we toil for a harvest; in contemplation the Master of prayer comes to us and serves us, giving the grace of contemplation as pure gift. The first three stages are active, the last passive. In the first three we, like farmhands, take up a task, while in contemplation we are taken up ... by Love.

Spiritual writers compare meditation to rowing a sailboat and contemplation to sailing, carried on by the wind of the Spirit. The first three steps up Jacob's ladder require arduous effort, whereas the last rung gives rest and repose. As we make our way in the spiritual life, trudging up what seems like an endless incline, we cannot forget the thrill of what awaits us at the top. It is for good reason that the ascent up a steep ladder is one of the favorite images for the journey to God.

While it is pure gift, it shouldn't surprise us that contemplation is not as common or easy at the outset of the Christian walk.

Contemplation is the fruit and experience of love; it takes time, like cultivating a vine in order to sip a complex wine. We must be trained to love, and if we have not love, we cannot have contemplation. I suspect that as we grow in faith and love for God the moments and occasions of contemplation likewise grow: moving from an intense but momentary experience to one that grows as our capacity to love grows. We can all be contemplatives, provided that our gaze is kindled by love.

Moving Beyond Words

As already noted, one of the difficulties of discussing *contemplatio* is that it is—by design—something that takes us past words and into the experience of the love and joy of God Himself. So *contemplatio* exists at the border of, and often well beyond, what language can do. As an illustration of this, consider one of the greatest poets of the nineteenth century, Fr. Gerard Manley Hopkins. In his journal entry for August 18, 1874, he recounts a seemingly small incident: "As we drove home the stars came out thick: I leant back to look at them and my heart opening more than usual praised Our Lord to and in whom all that beauty comes home."

We read this and think, "How nice. What a pious thought." And move on.

But when Hopkins applies the full weight of his intense poetic genius to the same incident, we get this unexpected explosion of glorious poetry:

> Look at the stars! Look, look up at the skies!
> O look at all the fire-folk sitting in the air!
> The Bright boroughs, the circle-citadels there!

> Down in dim woods the diamond delves! The elves'-eyes
> The grey lawns cold where gold, where quickgold lies!
> Wind-beat whitebeam! Airy abeles set on a flare!
> Flake-doves sent floating forth at a farmyard scare!—
> Ah well! It is all a purchase, all is a prize.
> Buy then! Bid then! — What? — Prayer, patience,
> alms, vows.
> Look, look: a May-mess, like on orchard boughs!
> Look! March-boom, like on mealed-with-yellow sallows!
> These are indeed the barn; withindoors house
> The shocks. This piece-bright paling shuts the spouse
> Christ home, Christ and his mother and all his hallows.

Mere prose only hinted at the titanic feelings of joy, wonder, and gratitude surging below the surface of that journal entry. As poet Margaret Smith has noted,[25] the curious thing about Hopkins (and I would argue, about all of us) is that the closer we get to speaking what is truly in our hearts, the less possible it becomes to say it in prose (and, ultimately, to say it at all). Our words want to take flight, to become poetry or, better still, music.

So, when lovers propose marriage, they seldom approach the beloved saying, "It has come to my attention that we seem to be physically and mentally compatible. I would therefore like to request that you enter into a permanent arrangement of shared socio-economic resources with me for the purpose of providing mutual psycho-social and economic support, as well as breeding future members of our species." Nor would the beloved be pleased if he did. What the moment demands is poetry or, better still, music. The beauty and glory of love

---

[25] Margaret Smith, *A Holy Struggle: Unspoken Thoughts of Hopkins* (Wheaton, IL: Harold Shaw, 1992).

calls for dramatic gestures like kneeling in public. It calls us to sing things such as:

> Arise, my love, my fair one,
> and come away;
> for lo, the winter is past,
> the rain is over and gone.
> The flowers appear on the earth,
> the time of singing has come,
> and the voice of the turtledove is heard in our land.
> The fig tree puts forth its figs,
> and the vines are in blossom; they give forth fragrance.
> Arise, my love, my fair one,
> and come away (Sng 2:10-13).

The point of *lectio divina* is to lead us into an encounter with the most glorious love in the universe, the love that unites Christ the Bridegroom with His Bride the Church (cf. Eph 5:21 and following). So it should be no surprise that meditation on this reality bears the rich fruit of contemplation, not unlike the poetry of the Song of Songs. Contemplation *feels*.

But because contemplation leads us to the boundaries of what language can express (and sometimes well beyond), we should not be surprised to find that language used by contemplatives trying to describe the experience of contemplation can often be, by turns, confusing or daunting. It may seem, like Hopkins' journal entry, strangely inadequate for describing the depths of the experience. As inadequate as the language may seem, it is amazing how earthy and concrete the language of the contemplative is. It is language, like that of the psalmist, about things which you can see, feel, and smell. Contemplation does not require us to try to look beyond or away from this world, but rather to look into the depths of creation and find within it its mystery and its Maker.

Contemplatio: A Gift of Grace

There can be a tendency (especially among beginners) to despair at this point. We are, after all, no Thomas Aquinas or John of the Cross or Teresa of Avila. So what hope can there possibly be of me arriving at such sublime heights as these great ones? The great news of the gospel is this: You *do* have hope that *God will grant you* the gift of *contemplatio*. Because that's what it is: a gift, and not an achievement.

In other words, *contemplatio* cannot be attained by human effort alone. It is *always* a gift of grace that depends on the movement of the Holy Spirit, not on our cleverness or will-power. On the other hand, *contemplatio* is not something wholly unrelated to what we do. On the contrary, it is the fruit of all our labor and openness to the Holy Spirit and His promptings in *lectio, meditatio,* and *oratio.*

If this sounds strange, it shouldn't. We see much the same thing in other aspects of life. The musician whose music transfigures an ordinary moment with heart-piercing beauty is likewise a sort of lightning rod for grace. But how did she get to be that way? She didn't just "luck out." She became a fine musician by learning her craft through years of hard work, steady practice and study. The man with the happy marriage and wonderful children is likewise a recipient of grace. But, again, he is not simply inexplicably fortunate. He has that family also because he was seeking virtue in his choice of a spouse and because he spent long steady years on a million small acts of love for his wife and children that cooperated with grace to build that marriage and those kids. The master writer who crafts a tale shot through with beauty that wrings the heart, the deep-thinking philosopher whose insights illuminate the soul with the truth and beauty of God; none of them could bear the smallest fruit without the grace of God. But none of them do what they do by "dumb luck." They do it because they have applied themselves to developing skill and pursuing virtue in their fields and have been, in time, rewarded with the grace they sought.

Dante hints at this truth in Canto 33 of *Paradise* in his *Divine Comedy*. He has told us the tale of his journey through hell, then up Mount Purgatory, and through all the circles of heaven, all in search of God. But when the moment comes where he encounters God in the image of the Celestial Rose, words fail him at last:

> As the geometer who sets himself
> To square the circle and who cannot find,
> For all his thought, the principle he needs,
> Just so was I on seeing this new vision
> I wanted to see how our image fuses
> Into the circle and finds its place in it,
> Yet my wings were not meant for such a flight –
> Except that then my mind was struck by lightning
> Through which my longing was at last fulfilled.
> Here powers failed my high imagination:
> But by now my desire and will were turned,
> Like a balanced wheel rotated evenly,
> By the Love that moves the sun and the other stars.[26]

The point is this: We can't *make* lightning strike. We can't make the longing of our lives be fulfilled. But we can do our part to make sure the lightning rod is well-placed and made of copper instead of wood.

---

[26] Dante Alighieri, *Divine Comedy: Paradiso*, trans. James Finn Cotter (New York: Lilian Barber, 1988), Canto XXXIII.

When it does strike, it is a pure gift of grace. But it is a gift of grace which we have sought and for which we have readied ourselves by a long and steady attendance to the Word of God and obedience to His will.

One Step at a Time

Contemplation is an act of love and also its fruit. Therefore, it should be no more confined to convents and cloisters than love itself. Contemplation is a universal calling, and Scripture counsels that in responding to that call we should walk one step at a time, looking neither to the right nor the left (Dt 5:32), and not worrying about tomorrow (Mt 6:34). Life in Christ is described as a "walk" not as a frantic hurry (Eph 5:2). We look at the witness of the saints, not to drag us down in despair, but to remind us that if they made it, so can we! That's why Hebrews 12:1-2 says:

> Therefore, since we are surrounded by so great a cloud of witnesses, let us also lay aside every weight, and sin which clings so closely, and let us run with perseverance the race that is set before us, looking to Jesus the pioneer and perfecter of our faith, who for the joy that was set before him endured the cross, despising the shame, and is seated at the right hand of the throne of God.

The saints are the athletes who have already run the race and are now in the stands, cheering for us and urging us on to victory in Christ, too.

One of the greatest of these saints, Thérèse of Lisieux, struggled like most of us with the belief that she could never measure up to the saints in the spiritual Big Leagues. Her wise elder sister taught her a new way of seeing things:

One day I expressed surprise that God does not give an equal amount of glory to all the elect in Heaven—I was afraid that they would not all be quite happy. She sent me to fetch Papa's big tumbler, and put it beside my tiny thimble, then, filling both with water, she asked me which seemed the fuller. I replied that one was as full as the other—it was impossible to pour more water into either of them, for they could not hold it. In this way Pauline made it clear to me that in Heaven the least of the Blessed does not envy the happiness of the greatest; and so, by bringing the highest mysteries down to the level of my understanding, she gave my soul the food it needed.[27]

This is sound advice for those practicing *lectio divina*. Our business is not to worry about how the experience of *contemplatio* will come to us, nor to fret about how we are doing in comparison to our neighbor in the pew, let alone the spiritual giants in our tradition.

Instead, we should simply pray "Give us this day our daily bread," and like Lazarus' sister Mary sit faithfully at the feet of our Lord through regular practice of *lectio divina*. Growing in spiritual maturity is like growing in physical maturity; what is new is often difficult, but facility comes with continual practice and repetition. As you become acquainted with Scripture through the steady practice of *lectio*, you imperceptibly come to know Scripture as a familiar family story. The connections, parallels, and echoes between various biblical passages and stories intertwine like the vines of the vineyard. What at first may

---

[27] St. Thérèse of Lisieux, *The Autobiography of St. Thérèse of Lisieux With Additional Writings and Sayings of St. Thérèse,* trans. Thomas N. Taylor (Available on-line at http://infomotions.com/etexts/gutenberg/dirs/1/6/7/7/16772/16772.htm as of August 25, 2008.)

have seemed like walking through a confusing labyrinth, now feels like the familiar walkways of a beautiful garden. You discover that the books of Scripture aren't just read. They are read and re-read. It is by reading Luke 50 times that it matures like a fine wine. It is consistent and habitual reading of the Bible that brings the realization that you are just seeing the tip of the iceberg.

This means, by the way, that *contemplatio* is not a plateau you climb to and then kick down the ladder of four rungs. The grace of *contemplatio* is the wind of the Spirit: it blows where it wills (Jn 3:8). But like all God's grace, it is given not to replace our efforts but to inspire our efforts. The musician who, after long practice, plays her first truly beautiful piece does not then declare that she no longer needs to work at her craft. The sailor who has to labor to row his boat out into the wind does not declare that he will never need to row again, nor work to trim the sails and helm the boat. In the same way, *lectio divina* does not end when *contemplatio* is given us. Rather, that grace is granted to inspire us to still greater application to the Word of God.

The Word must always be made flesh, and so contemplation must lead to deeds of love. The labor of *lectio, meditatio,* and *oratio* comes to a climax in the arousal of love that *contemplatio* names, and that love spills over into action. That is why we must now turn to *operatio*.

Chapter Seven

Operatio

But be doers of the word, and not hearers only, deceiving yourselves. For if any one
is a hearer of the word and not a doer, he is like a man who observes his natural
face in a mirror; for he observes himself and goes away and at once forgets what he
was like. But he who looks into the perfect law, the law of liberty, and perseveres,
being no hearer that forgets but a doer that acts, he shall be blessed in his doing.
— James 1:22-25

To build your life on Christ, to accept His word with joy and put its teachings
into practice. This, young people of the third millennium, should be your program.
— Pope Benedict XVI

Readers familiar with classical discussions of *lectio divina* will note that this chapter is, so to speak, adding an extra "rung" to the ladder. This is true, but I make no apologies. In fact, such additions are not wholly without precedent. For example, some who practice *lectio divina* within group settings add a step called *collatio* (discussion). Other spiritual writers have added a "rung" before *lectio* called *statio* (position) that emphasizes the importance of creating a quiet and prayerful place for the prayer. By including this fifth and final step, I do so not to innovate or "improve" upon the Catholic tradition, but to make plain for a modern reader what would have simply been assumed by a medieval reader: namely, that for the careful cultivation of *lectio divina* to really bear fruit that lasts (Jn 15:16), it must result in a life of virtue. The Word must be "made flesh" again and again in our daily lives.

As the passage from James cited above makes clear, the Church has always insisted that the real way to show your faith in Christ is not merely to profess it, but to prove it through tangible actions. By living out the faith we begin to build "habits of virtue." Indeed, Peter exhorted the first Christians to "make every effort to supplement your faith with virtue" (2 Pt 1:5). Thus, our final stage in this process of prayer is *operatio*.

Making the Gospel Second Nature

Some people have the notion that "habits" are dull and difficult, a hindrance to the freedom and spontaneity that they imagine must come with being truly "spiritual." But in fact, habits make us free, and spontaneity can often be a prison. Show me a music pupil who will not practice but insists on playing "how I feel," and I will show you a music student who never learns to play anything very well. Show me a child who has not had parents who drilled "Please" and "Thank You" and "Wash Your Hands" into him or her until they are habitual, and I will show you a child imprisoned in selfish rudeness whose horizons for friendship, creativity, and even a happy life are radically limited. The piano student who develops the habit of practice eventually reaches the point where he knows the keyboard so well that he is free to play what he pleases. Similarly, when you first learn to drive, it's hard work and engrossing, but once the habits of a good driver are formed, you are free to think about other things and talk to others as you drive (just as long as you keep your eye on the road). In every case, good habits free us. It is only bad habits that enslave us.

We speak of good habits as being "second nature" to us. In the case of the Christian life, this is not mere metaphor, for Scripture tells us that we are "partakers of the divine nature" (2 Pt 1:4) when we are "born from on high" in baptism. And the purpose of the sacraments is to instill grace in us and strengthen us so that we can live out the life of the Blessed Trinity. The key to all this is incarnation: making the Word incarnate in our lives by actually obeying Jesus and imitating Him. And the point is in the doing, not merely in thinking or feeling.

In *The Screwtape Letters* by C.S. Lewis, Uncle Screwtape, a distinguished bureaucrat in the "lowerarchy" of hell, writes advice to his nephew Wormwood, a junior tempter out in the field who is trying to damn his first human soul. Within this dialogue we are treated to a view of the life of grace from the perspective of hell, where God is "the Enemy" and Satan is "Our Father Below." In Screwtape's upside-down universe, the hellish perspective on the moral life is revealed:

> Think of your man as a series of concentric circles, his will being the innermost, his intellect coming next, and finally his fantasy. You can hardly hope, at once, to exclude from all the circles everything that smells of the Enemy: but you must keep on shoving all the virtues outward till they are finally located in the circle of fantasy, and all the desirable qualities inward into the Will. It is only in so far as they reach the will and are there embodied in habits that the virtues are really fatal to us.[28]

The last thing the devil wants us to do is put into practice any

---

[28] C.S. Lewis, *The Screwtape Letters* (New York: HarperCollins, 2001), p. 28.

insights or guidance we might receive from God in *lectio divina*. If he can keep us merely thinking, or better yet simply fantasizing, about the faith, or feeling good about it, he is quite content.

Virtue that is merely approved but not practiced is essentially worthless. In fact, it can be delusional and dangerous. The Pharisees, after all, approved of virtue; but they did not practice it. This is why Jesus offers us a warning:

> Not every one who says to me, "Lord, Lord," shall enter the kingdom of heaven, but he who does the will of my Father who is in heaven. On that day many will say to me, "Lord, Lord, did we not prophesy in your name, and cast out demons in your name, and do many mighty works in your name?" And then will I declare to them, "I never knew you; depart from me, you evildoers." Every one then who hears these words of mine and does them will be like a wise man who built his house upon the rock; and the rain fell, and the floods came, and the winds blew and beat upon that house, but it did not fall, because it had been founded on the rock. And every one who hears these words of mine and does not do them will be like a foolish man who built his house upon the sand; and the rain fell, and the floods came, and the winds blew and beat against that house, and it fell; and great was the fall of it (Mt 7:21-27).

Only one thing is necessary, as Jesus said to Martha: to hear the Word of God and do it.

But we seem to have a genius for missing that truth. We can, for instance, hear the Word and speculate about it, but not do it. We can hear the Word and feel really good about it, but not do it. We can hear the Word and provide a complete analysis of it, but not do it. We can hear the Word and tell others about it, but not do it. We can hear the Word and tell ourselves we will get right on that, and not do it. We can do many things out of distraction and not put into practice the Word of God. None of these things will build habits of virtue. Hearing the Word of God and doing it is what builds habits of virtue, which enables us to love in action, not just in word.

Making Meditation Fruitful

If we think back to some of our previous reflections on Scripture in this book we can easily see moments where what we have found in *lectio, meditatio,* and *oratio* can be applied to our own life. For instance, in the story of Mary and Martha it is easy—indeed, it is almost inevitable—that we should begin to ask, "Am I more like Mary or Martha?" That's the sort of thing to be brought to God in *oratio.* And as you reflect, you may, for instance, be moved to sit down and write a list of the "many things" that are distracting you as they distracted Martha. You may want to ask God if there is some practical way you can sit at Jesus' feet and listen better. Perhaps there is somebody else in your life that needs to have that time and space in their life and God is calling you to help them. Maybe as you go to God in prayer on what the "one thing necessary" in your life may be, you are moved to ask God how you in your specific circumstances can "seek first his kingdom" as He commands. Perhaps you are afraid to trust God that "all these things will be added as well" and you need to talk to Him about that fear of letting go of earthly things for the sake of heavenly ones. But our response to God regarding these movements of our heart cannot be in word only.

In my own life, I have found that adding this fifth rung to the ladder—*operatio*—has been astonishingly helpful in making *lectio divina* more fruitful in my life. I discovered this principle with the help of my spiritual director, who encouraged me to make, at the end of my prayer time, a concrete resolution which I would strive to put into action during that day so as to focus my energies on living out the Lord's Word. My director pointed out to me the following striking and insightful quote from St. Francis de Sales' *Introduction to the Devout Life.*

> ABOVE all things, my daughter, strive when your meditation is ended to retain the thoughts and resolutions you have made as your earnest practice throughout the day. This is the real fruit of meditation, without which it is apt to be unprofitable, if not actually harmful—inasmuch as to dwell upon virtues without practicing them lends to puff us up with unrealities, until we begin to fancy ourselves all that we have meditated upon and resolved to be; which is all very well if our resolutions are earnest and substantial, but on the contrary hollow and dangerous if they are not put in practice. You must then diligently endeavor to carry out your resolutions, and seek for all opportunities, great or small. For instance, if your resolution was to win over those who oppose you by gentleness, seek through the day any occasion of meeting such persons kindly, and if none offers, strive to speak well of them, and pray for them.[29]

Wow. St. Francis de Sales warns that prayer and meditation can be spiritually dangerous! If we spend time meditating and learning

---

[29] St. Francis De Sales, *Introduction to the Devout Life*, Part II, Chapter 8, "Some Useful Hints as to Meditation."

about holiness and virtue, the danger is that we will think we have acquired these qualities simply because we have thought about them, when in reality and practice we have yet to attain them.

St. Francis De Sales is simply reiterating the teaching of Scripture: "What does it profit, my brethren, if a man says he has faith but has not works? Can his faith save him? If a brother or sister is ill-clad and in lack of daily food, and one of you says to them, 'Go in peace, be warmed and filled,' without giving them the things needed for the body, what does it profit? So faith by itself, if it has no works, is dead" (Jas 2:14-17). Daily resolutions ground us in reality, and help burst the inflated balloon of our pride, which has an amazing propensity to self-inflate.

Target a Particular Virtue

The first challenge I found in adding a practical resolution at the conclusion of my prayer was remembering to make a resolution at all. And even when I did make a resolution I found that I soon forgot what my resolution had been. So I decided to try something new to help jump-start my *operatio*. I started to write down my resolutions in my small notebook that I carry with me during the day. I made resolutions on everything from offering a sacrifice by changing my diet, to loving my son by committing to go bike riding with him every morning before work, to helping my wife in small things. (She will read this so I can't claim too much!)

And do you know what? It didn't seem to work! It did, however, document how many resolutions I broke and didn't act upon. I found after the first week that I had accomplished no more than two days worth of resolutions! But I pressed on. And as I did, I found that growth in Christ was something like learning to ice skate. You fall down and you get up; that's natural in learning how to ice skate. It's just how it goes. But as you keep getting up you get a little bit more coordinated, a little more graceful, a little stronger, and a little more confident. If you resolve to learn ice-skating, regardless of how long it takes and how difficult it is, then you will fall and get up and learn to ice skate. If you resolve to learn ice-skating while never falling, you will both fall and *not* learn to ice-skate.

It's the same with the spiritual life. You *will* fall down. Nothing will help you grow in humility like writing down your daily resolutions and then going over them at the end of the day and reviewing them at the end of the week. But then you can go to the sacrament of reconciliation and ask Jesus to help you get back up and start practicing again. Little by little, the concrete resolutions, the conquest of bad habits and the acquisition of good habits set us free. Small resolutions, over time, can lead to huge revolutions affecting not only our lives but also the lives of those around us. It may mean repeating resolutions over and over again, at least if you are like me. Follow this through and you might unleash hidden talents and gifts you had buried. And in so doing, you might call forth similar gifts in your kids or friends.

St. Francis de Sales gives another helpful suggestion about our resolutions. He tells us to be specific:

> But, my daughter, you must not stop short in general affections, without turning them into special resolutions for your own correction and amendment. For instance, meditating on Our Dear Lord's First Word from the Cross, you will no doubt be roused to the desire of

imitating Him in forgiving and loving your enemies. But that is not enough, unless you bring it to some practical resolution, such as, "I will not be angered any more by the annoying things said of me by such or such a neighbor, nor by the slights offered me by such a one; but rather I will do such and such things in order to soften and conciliate them." In this way, my daughter, you will soon correct your faults, whereas mere general resolutions would take but a slow and uncertain effect.[30]

Much depends on how you make the resolution. To take aim at a good resolution it is often best to use a riflescope rather than a shotgun approach. Pinpoint specific things you can do to grow in a virtue. One of my greatest challenges is being organized. I used to make resolutions to "be better organized," but they never seemed to work. Following St. Francis de Sales, I saw that this resolution was too general. What I needed was to drill down and get concrete: clean up my desk before leaving work, put paperwork in its proper place, answer emails within forty-eight hours, and many other specific resolutions that I fail to keep more often than not. It is a battle to improve. And even if we never fully achieve the virtue we strive for, at least the struggle will help us gain humility!

The vital thing is to go after a particular virtue and pursue it with relentless regularity. Don't just aim at being good, holy, or loving, but think of how love is embodied in your particular circumstances. Perhaps there is a difficult person you need to win over with gentleness and heroic patience. God fills our life with fallen people so that we can practice heroic virtue and become holy.

---

[30] St. Francis De Sales, *Introduction to the Devout Life*, Part II, Chapter 6, "The Third Part of Meditation, Affections and Resolutions."

Where to Start in Scripture

What part of the Bible should you start reading for *lectio divina*? I suggest that you begin with the gospels. The gospels of Luke or John are, in my opinion, the easiest place to start, but you can't go wrong starting with Matthew and Mark. After the gospels, I recommend the book of Psalms. The psalms were the staple of the Desert Fathers and the monks. If you are in the habit of attending daily Mass, then you might use one of the readings from Mass. You may also want to pray the Liturgy of the Hours, the official prayer of the Church, which is largely based on the Scripture readings the Church uses every day. You can get an easy-to-use version that contains all the Scripture texts for Mass and Morning and Evening Prayer for each day of the month from Magnificat (www.magnificat.com). I often take one of the psalms used in the Morning Prayer of the day for my *lectio*.

After the gospels and psalms, move on to the letters of St. Paul. After these, any book of the Bible is fair game. But no matter what books of the Bible you read and what reading plan you follow, you should always return to the gospels on a regular basis, as this is the Catholic tradition followed by the monks. It is a good idea to read through one (or more) of the four gospels at least once a year.

Once you begin reading Scripture regularly, I highly recommend the *Great Adventure Bible Timeline* reading plan, which will take you through the fourteen narrative books of the Bible and help you understand the overall story of Scripture. There is also a series of *Great Adventure* Bible studies on specific books of the Bible, such as Matthew, Acts, Revelation, Exodus, 1 Corinthians, James, with more to come. This is an excellent way to begin a deeper study of Scripture, and a deeper understanding of Scripture and its story will fuel deeper *lectio,* and the fruit will be a richer *lectio divina* and prayer life.

Practical Suggestions

What translation of the Bible should you use? The best translation is the one you are going to be most comfortable with and which you will use the most. The New American Bible is used in the liturgy in the United States, but for study I recommend the RSV-CE (Revised Standard Version–Catholic Edition). Avoid the NRSV (New Revised Standard Version), due to numerous translation problems (e.g., Daniel's "Son of Man" is translated as "human being," thereby missing the messianic title that is key to Jesus' use of the same phrase.) The Jerusalem Bible is another excellent translation. No matter which version you use, though, make sure you are comfortable with the translation, because if you don't like it, you won't read it as much as you should!

I also recommend that you keep a notebook with your Bible for your *lectio.* You can write down key points from your meditation, and furthermore you can record your resolutions and keep track of how well you put them into practice. I use a small moleskin notebook that fits in my pocket so that I can take it everywhere.

Therefore, your first resolution should be to get a good Bible (if you don't already have one) and a notebook. Next, choose your time and place and start praying with Scripture. *Lectio divina* is a method that won't grow old. As St. Gregory the Great once observed, as we grow, our reading of Scripture grows too. The Word is ever ancient, ever new. May it renew and nourish you!

Transformation in Christ: What It's All About

If you have read this far, it is probably a safe assumption that you are going to give *lectio divina* a serious shot. I encourage you to "keep your eye on the prize."

St. Paul encouraged the early Christians to persevere, saying "God is at work in you, both to will and to work for his good pleasure" (Phil 2:13). Practicing *lectio divina*, and being faithful to it, is hard work. But if you persevere, you will discover that God will work in your life and you will witness your own transformation, albeit slowly, into an icon of Jesus Christ. When we put out the effort to read, to meditate, to pray, to open ourselves to the gift of contemplation, and above all to hear the Word of God and do it, God answers us with gifts beyond what we could ever imagine or achieve on our own. We don't "earn" the grace of God. Indeed, we never would be able to even try without the grace of God already at work in us. But we do labor in the vineyard with faith that God will give the increase and that by drinking the wine of the Word in both Scripture and sacrament we shall at length stand before Him "with unveiled face, beholding the glory of the Lord … changed into his likeness from one degree of glory to another; for this comes from the Lord who is the Spirit" (2 Cor 3:18).

Index

About the Author

Dr. Tim Gray is the president of the Augustine Institute, a Catholic graduate school in Scripture and Evangelization, and professor of Scripture at St. John Vianney Seminary in Denver. He has authored several books, including *Jesus and the Temple*, *Mission of the Messiah*, *Sacraments in Scripture*, and serves as co-author of one of the leading Catholic Bible Study programs, *The Great Adventure Bible Study Series*. Dr. Gray is a nationally renowned speaker and is a regular host on the Eternal Word Television Network (EWTN). He holds a doctorate in biblical studies from Catholic University of America, as well as master's degrees in Scripture from Duke University and theology from Franciscan University of Steubenville. He resides in Denver with his wife, Kris, and son, Joseph.